The Spiritual Wheel of GOD

Learning How to Understand and Implement Your Spiritual Gifts

Jacqueline Parker Scott, EdD, MBA

Other Books authored by Jacqueline Parker Scott, EdD, MBA

Spiritual Awakening: Look What Happened to Me. Is it Happening to You Too?

Super Parenting: Raising The Next Generation
Co-authored with daughter, Olympia Scott, 2-time WNBA Champion

The Spiritual Wheel of GOD

Learning How to Understand and Implement Your Spiritual Gifts

Jacqueline Parker Scott, EdD, MBA

O and J Awakenings
2022

First Printing: 2022

ISBN 978-0-9906644-2-0

O and J Awakenings
PO Box 45261
Los Angeles, CA 90045

www.MySpiritualAwakenings.com

Ordering Information:

Special discounts are available on quantity purchases by churches, corporations, associations, educators, and others. For details, contact the publisher at info@myspiritualawakenings.com.

Dedication

In memory of my parents,
Thomas Aubrey Parker Sr.
and Daisy Singleton Parker

In memory of my daughter,
Tres Mali Scott

My children,
Olympia and Stephen

My grandchildren,
BreAzia, Rachman, Jr., Walter, Logann, Makailah, and Micaiah

My brothers and sisters,
Harriet, Tonette, Thomas, Jr., Joseph,
Gale, April, and Pastor Renee

Table of Contents

Preface

This book teaches you how to use your spiritual gift(s) from the Holy Spirit. It is designed to help people understand their spiritual gifts and the responsibility that comes with it. It will help you learn how to treat your spiritual gifts seriously and effectively.

Everyone has spiritual gifts, but you must want them and be obedient to the Lord so He can work through you as a vessel. It is not you but the Father above who does it all. Jesus Christ does all the work. The Holy Spirit uses your energy to perform the miracles here on Earth.

Jesus told me I would write this book to help His people learn how to use their spiritual gifts. He gave me the ten lessons of the Spiritual Wheel of GOD. In this context, "GOD" stands for the "Gifts of Development. I refer to this throughout the book as the "Spiritual Gifts of Development." This book was written by Jesus Christ through me. I am so blessed and honored that Jesus chose me to be His vessel for this book.

As Jesus gave me the information for this book, He used my testimonies to help His people understand the concepts that He presented to them. He keeps the Bible live in modern-day times. We are living the Bible over and over, generation after generation. And the Lord allowed me to be a part of His demonstrations. Thank you, Jesus.

As I was writing this book with Jesus Christ, I continued to tell my stories through my testimonies. The testimonies in this book are true events that happened in my life, which demonstrate how I use my spiritual gifts that Jesus Christ gave to me.

Everyone has a ministry to serve God's people. You are either a minister on the pulpit or a minister among the people as one of the people. I am a minister among the people as one of the people. Jesus Christ reiterated my ministry to me as I put pen to paper. During my morning prayers on October 7, 2015, Jesus said to me:

Your ministry is to teach My people how to perform their spiritual gifts. You will write books to teach many souls all over the world. They will read your books and learn a lot from them.

Your ministry as a prophet is to help people with their problems in coping with the flesh. You will help many save their souls.

Many of you will have personal testimonies to tell, your own spiritual gifts. If you do not have them yet, don't worry. Just the fact that you are reading this book means there is more to come to you in the spiritual realm.

Jesus Christ allowed me to interject parts of my life into this book, both my supernatural and spiritual life, with Him. I am baptized in the spirit. I have a very special relationship with Jesus Christ. I accept Him into my heart as my Lord and Savior. He leads me and guides me step by step. I do not worry. I know that Jesus loves me, takes care of me, protects me, provides for me, and He is with me 24/7.

Jesus told me to write this book and gave me the title of the book in 2013. He told me to finish it at the end of 2015. The book was completed in 2016 and published in 2022.

Introduction

While many of us want spiritual gifts, do we really understand the responsibility that comes along with it? We must understand that our spiritual gifts are to be used for God's people. They are not to be used to prophesize in a grandiose, self-egotistical earthly manner. In other words, the gifts are not for you to use for your own self-gratification.

The spiritual gifts are holy gifts and should be treated as such. There are nine spiritual gifts: wisdom, knowledge, faith, healing, mighty deeds, prophecy, discernment, tongues, and interpretation of tongues (1 Cor. 12:8–10).

The nine spiritual gifts are used to help serve God's people. Everyone has spiritual gifts; they are distributed to each of us as the Holy Spirit so desires (1 Cor. 12:11). God gives spiritual gifts to all of us for our service. Your spiritual gifts help you with your personal purpose, ministry, and destiny. Pray for God to reveal your spiritual gift(s) to you if you do not already know.

When you pray for spiritual gifts, it needs to be for the right reason. The gift of tongues is very special. It allows your spirit to pray directly to God without any interference. Some people pray to receive the gift of tongues for the wrong reasons, such as showing others how holy they are. Your spiritual gifts are a gift from God and should be used and treated as a special thing.

The purpose of this book is twofold. Once you receive your spiritual gift(s), you will need to learn how to nurture it and serve your gift to God's people as He desires. You are God's vessel. It is the Father above. It is Jesus Christ who does all the work.

Second, the book is written how Jesus instructed me to write it. I have provided excerpts from my memoirs on how Jesus orchestrated it. Everyone can learn from this book, including me! I have learned so much from Jesus' guidance and have benefited greatly from it.

On the morning of July 11, 2015, I was blessed with an idea that came directly from Jesus Christ that spurred the concept of this book. Every morning, I sit up in my bed that overlooks the front yard where there are beautiful trees and birds chirping. I say my prayers, and then I open up my heart to hear Jesus' message. I hear His messages through thoughts. It's just like when you think of something you have to do, and you can hear that thought in your mind. That self-talk is the communication method Jesus uses with me. I always document what Jesus says or what I feel on my laptop, and it's a good way for me to look back and reflect on my own spiritual journey.

On that particular day, it felt like the world had shifted. Jesus had spoken to me, and I immediately knew that what He was telling me was going to be part of something bigger. Jesus Christ created the Spiritual Gifts of Development, which is also known as the Spiritual Wheel of GOD. Below is an excerpt from my memoirs when Jesus spoke to me:

July 11, 2015
Morning prayers

"Good morning, Jesus. What do you have to say to me today?"

In your book, you will develop the Spiritual Gifts of Development [the Spiritual Wheel of GOD]. The spokes of the wheel will branch out to the lessons. In the middle of the wheel, there will be God [the Holy Spirit] who is sending and receiving messages and giving directions on how to develop your gift(s).

The wheel moves among His people. It is constantly moving because things are constantly changing. It is a moving, living wheel. To perform your gifts well, you must understand the ten lessons of the Spiritual Gifts of Development. Those lessons are within the Spiritual Wheel of GOD.

After my prayers, I sat back and read what I had typed, and I could not believe it! Jesus had given me such an important message. I thought about His words, visualizing what He had said, and it all became so clear in my head. As a result of Jesus' guidance, I have visualized what He wanted me to share with the world: The Spiritual Wheel of GOD (see Figure 1 on the next page).

Isn't that such a beautiful thing? The Spiritual Wheel of GOD! There are so many lessons we can learn from Jesus! Just like we have a mental weapon of protection against evil with the Armor of God, we have a mental tool to use in a metaphor for understanding and implementing our spiritual gifts.

Jesus explained the lessons in my morning prayers in 2013 prior to revealing the Spiritual Gifts of Development, or the Spiritual Wheel of GOD, in 2015, giving me the understanding that the lessons are the spokes in the Spiritual Wheel. Below is an excerpt from my memoirs when Jesus spoke to me:

December 14, 2013
Morning prayers

"Good morning, dear Jesus. Do you have anything to say?"

Yes. You will briefly go over all of the lessons [the spokes in the Spiritual Wheel of GOD] and make brief statements of what it is like and share with people about your own spiritual awakening. After you go over the ten lessons and the summary, you will ask those who have received their spiritual gifts during the ten lessons to write a statement of what it meant to them to go through the lessons and actually receive their gifts. You will include them in your book. It will be fascinating to the members to be a part of your second book.

At the prayer group meeting that night, I relayed Jesus' message about the ten lessons. After the meeting, I took the members aside individually and asked what they thought about what I had said in the prayer meeting. One of the prayer members told me that she had received the gift of prophecy during the prayer meeting. (See the Appendixes for a detailed account written by the prayer member who received the gift of prophecy, as well as written accounts of my prayer partner and myself.)

In your quest for spiritual awakening, you must understand how spiritual gifts work. Not only do you have to understand how they work, but you must also know how to implement them. You will need to know when and how. Timing is everything. When the Lord Jesus Christ revealed to me the ten spokes of the Spiritual Wheel of GOD, I knew I needed to get to work. In this book, I discuss the ten lessons to develop your spiritual gift(s). The first five lessons (Part I) deal with understanding spiritual gifts, and the last five lessons (Part II) deal with implementing them.

Below is the summary of the ten lessons that Jesus gave me about the Spiritual Wheel of GOD. I wrote down Jesus' words and how He addressed me:

In Lesson 1 [the first spoke], you will talk about preparation for the gifts. You will need to prepare yourself so that you are ready to receive them. You will tell your testimony of when evil snatched your spirit out of your body.

In Lesson 2 [the second spoke], you will talk about God's people. The spiritual gifts are for God's people, not for you. You minister to others and others minister to you. You will tell your testimony of when you locked your keys in the trunk of your car.

In Lesson 3 [the third spoke], you will talk about how God distributes His spiritual gifts according to His will. Some will have one gift, some will have few gifts, and some will have many gifts. You will tell your testimony of messages and when you healed your colleague's leg.

In Lesson 4 [the fourth spoke], you will talk about how you must have faith to receive your spiritual gifts. You will tell your testimony of your faith when you believed in yourself enough to deliver the first message, and you did as I commanded of you with a church greeter and healed her to walk without her cane.

In Lesson 5 [the fifth spoke], you will talk about the dedication to gifts. Once you receive them, you must be obedient and use your gifts wisely. You will tell your testimony of when you went to eight o'clock Mass on your day off to meet someone who never showed up.

In Lesson 6 [the sixth spoke], you will talk about how you need to work to help save souls. Your testimony will be about the times when you delivered messages to people who did not know you were going to deliver a message.

In Lesson 7 [the seventh spoke], you will talk about learning how to listen when the Lord speaks to you, whether it is the Holy Spirit or Jesus Himself. You must listen to what I have to say. You will give the testimonies of your assignments, spontaneity, and your casual talks with Me in asking questions.

In Lesson 8 [the eighth spoke], you will talk about obedience. You will talk about being consistent with obeying the Holy Spirit in what He tells you. You will give the testimony of how you delivered messages even though it was hard at times in the beginning.

In Lesson 9 [the ninth spoke], you will talk about everyone having a ministry on Earth. You will speak of your ministry and of others whom you know. You will explain how things you experience in life get you ready to do your ministry, the purpose of why you are here. You will give the testimony of your ministry and a few examples of others you have helped with their ministry.

In Lesson 10 [the tenth spoke], you will talk about spiritual warfare. You will explain about the spiritual battle and how one must always wear the spiritual Armor of God to protect oneself from evil. You will give your testimony when you were casting out of evil in the prayer meeting. You will talk about how you were shouted at and felt humiliated in front of the group for being obedient to God. You will talk about exorcism and deliverance.

I will guide you along the way. You are an educator, and you know how to develop curriculum. You were trained and educated to develop curriculum. You will continue to put your skills to good use.

Every chapter will discuss one spoke (one lesson) on the Spiritual Wheel of GOD. Every chapter is structured the same way. Here is a quick breakdown of how each chapter is structured:

At the beginning of each chapter, I provide a quick introduction about the lesson being discussed.

The next section is a list of scriptures that my prayer partner gave me in the order that she received them from the Holy Spirit. After that is a section of reflection about the scriptures where I invite you to reflect on the scriptures and how they resonate in your life. I would suggest writing down your findings in a journal.

In the next section I provide excerpts from my personal memoirs with Jesus Christ, as well as scenes from my prayer meetings where I communicate Jesus' lessons to my Charismatic prayer group meetings. The next section is a detailed account of my testimonies or someone else's. These are great examples for exploring what these lessons mean and how they are put into action.

Every lesson has seven keys, and every chapter provides an in-depth look at the seven keys. These keys are designed to further help you understand the specified lesson.

The chapter ends with a summary of all things discussed: scriptures, Friday prayer group meetings, memoir excerpts, testimonies, and the seven keys.

Finally, I would like to explain the timeline of this book. The lessons were introduced to the Charismatic prayer group members in the last quarter of 2013 on Friday evenings and continued into 2014. I started writing the book in 2015 with the expectations of completing and publishing by 2016/2017. The testimonies that illustrated points in the lessons can be dated anywhere from 2007 to 2014.

I have done my best to organize and structure the book in a way that makes sense. I've added headings and subheadings to help guide you along. All memoir excerpts are set off by the date. Please keep in mind that I am introducing the lessons to the members of the Charismatic prayer group on Friday evening meetings held at my church.

Whether you read this book on your own or if you are in a workshop, you will travel through the book seeking your true spiritual identity of the kingdom of God and purpose in life, or you will confirm what you already know.

After reading this book, you will have an understanding of each spiritual gift, every lesson that Jesus asked me to communicate to you, and how and when to use your spiritual gifts. I wish you well on your spiritual journey.

Part I: Understanding Spiritual Gifts

Chapter 1
Lesson 1: Preparation

"Now the very one who has prepared us for this very thing is God, who has given us the spirit as a first installment?" ~2 Corinthians 5:5

Preparation comes prior to receiving spiritual gifts. Keep in mind that spiritual gifts are irrevocable. There is no turning back. Responsibility comes with the spiritual gift. You must be prepared to take on the responsibility of your spiritual gift and perform the assignments as given.

Preparation is the first spoke in the Spiritual Wheel of GOD. God prepares you for your spiritual gift(s).

You will need to prepare yourself so that you are ready to receive your spiritual gift(s). In Lesson 1, I share the scriptures that Jesus gave to my spiritual partner in the order that she received them from the Holy Spirit.

After you go through the scriptures, you will venture into the Charismatic prayer group meetings of my experiences. Please note that the testimonies in this book are true experiences. I often use my memoirs to help tell the story of my testimonies.

In Lesson 1, I give my testimony of when evil snatched my spirit out of my body. Afterwards, I discuss the seven key points related to preparation for your spiritual gifts: The Holy Spirit, your spirit, humility, criticism, fasting, discipline, and surrendering.

The purpose of the scriptures is to set the tone for the lesson. When you read the scriptures, try to read them in a way that will resonate with your own purpose in life. Afterwards, I suggest writing down any thoughts in your journal.

The scriptures for this lesson show how you should live as Christians and as one body of Christ. The scriptures introduce the spiritual gifts that are irrevocable and identify the assignment of ministry to edify the body of Christ. The scriptures help you to look at how you should prepare yourself for the coming of the anointing of the spiritual gifts.

Scriptures for Preparation

> For the gifts and the calling of God are irrevocable . . . For of him and through Him and to Him are all things, to whom the glory forever. Amen . . . For as we have many members in one body, but all the members do not have the

same function, so we, being many, are one body in Christ, and individually members of one another. (Rom. 11:29, 36; Rom. 12:4–5)

Having then gifts differing according to the grace that is given to us, let us use them: if prophecy let us prophesy in proportion to our faith or ministry, let us use it in our ministering: he who teaches, in teaching; he who exhorts, in exhortation; he who gives, with liberality; he who leads, with diligence; he who shows mercy, with cheerfulness. (Rom. 12:6–8)

Let love be without hypocrisy. Abhor what is evil. Cling to what is good. Be kindly affectionate to one another with brotherly love, in honor giving preference to one another; not lagging in diligence, fervent in spirit, serving the Lord; rejoicing in hope, patience in tribulation, continuing steadfastly in prayer; distributing to the needs of the saints, given to hospitality. Bless those who prosecute you; bless and do not curse. Rejoice with those who rejoice, and weep with those who weep. (Rom. 12:9–15)

Be of the same mind with one another. Repay no one evil for evil. Have regard for the good things in the sight of all men. If it is possible, as much as depends on you, live peaceable with all men. (Rom. 12:16–18)

Beloved, do not avenge yourselves, but rather give to wrath, for it is written, Vengeance is Mine, I will repay, says the Lord. Therefore, if your enemy is hungry, feed him; If he is thirsty, give him a drink; For in so doing, you will heap burning coals of fire on his head. (Rom. 12:19–20)

Do not be overcome by evil but overcome evil with good. (Rom. 12:21)

I beseech you therefore, brethren, by the mercies of God, that you present your bodies a living sacrifice, holy and acceptable to God, which is your reasonable service. And do not be conformed to this world but be transformed by the renewing of your mind, that you may prove what is that is good and acceptable and perfect will of God. For I say through the grace given to me to everyone who is among you, not to think of himself more highly than he ought to think, but to think soberly, as God has dealt to each one a measure of faith. (Rom. 12:1–3)

Let every soul be subject to governing authorities. For there is no authority except from God, and the authorities that exist are appointed by God. (Rom. 13:1)

Therefore, whoever resists the authority resists the ordinance of God and those who resist will bring judgment on themselves. (Rom. 13:2)

For rulers are not a terror to good works, but to evil. Do you want to be unafraid of the authority? Do what is good, and you will have praise from the same. (Rom. 13.3)

For he is God's minister to you for good. But if you do evil, be afraid, for he does not bear the sword in vain, for he is God's minister an avenger to execute wrath on him who practices evil. (Rom. 13.4)

Therefore, you must be subject, not only because of wrath but also for conscience's sake. (Rom. 13:5)

For because of this you also pay taxes, for they are God's ministers attending continually to this very thing. Render therefore to all their due: taxes to whom taxes are due custom to whom customs, fear to whom fear, honor to whom honor. Owe no one anything except to love one another, for he who loves another has fulfilled the law. For the commandments, you shall not commit adultery, you shall not murder, you shall not steal, you shall not bear false witnesses, you shall not cover, and if there is any other commandment, are all summed up in this saying, namely, you shall love your neighbor as yourself. (Rom. 13:6–9)

Love does no harm to a neighbor: therefore, love is the fulfillment of the law. (Rom. 13:10)

Now concerning spiritual gifts brethren, I do not want you to be ignorant: You know that you were Gentiles, carried away to these dumb idols, however, you were led. Therefore, I make known to you that no one speaking by the Spirit of God calls Jesus accursed, and no one can say Jesus is Lord except by the Holy Spirit. There are diversities of gifts but the same spirit. There are differences of ministries but the same Lord. And there are diversities of activities but is the same God who works all in all. (1 Cor. 12:1–6)

But the manifestation of the spirit is given to each one for the profit of all. (1 Cor. 12:7)

For to one is given the word of wisdom through the Spirit, to another the word of knowledge through the same

Spirit, to another faith by the same Spirit, to another gifts of healing by the same Spirit, to another the workings of miracles, to another prophecy, to another discerning of Spirits, to another different kinds of tongues, to another the interpretation of tongues. (1 Cor. 12:8–10)

But one and the same Spirit works all these things, distributing to each one individually as He wills. For as the body is one and has many members, but all the members of that one body being many, are one body so also is Christ. For by one Spirit, we were all baptized into one body—whether Jews or Greeks, whether slaves or free—and have all been made to drink into one Spirit. (1 Cor. 12:11–13)

For in fact the body is not one member but many. If the foot should say, Because I am not a hand, I am not of the body, is it therefore not of the body? And if the ear should say, Because I am not an eye, I am not of the body, is it therefore not of the body? If the whole body were an eye, where would be the hearing? If the whole body were hearing, where would be the smelling? But now God has set the members, each one of them, in the body as He pleased. And if they were all one member, where would the body be? But now indeed there are many members, yet one body. And the eye cannot say to the hand, I have no need of you nor again the head to the feet, I have no need of you. No, much rather those members of the body which seem to be weaker are necessary. And those members of the body which we think to be less honorable on these we bestow greater honor; and our unpresentable parts have greater modesty, but our presentable parts have no need. But God composed the body having given greater honor to that part that lacks it; that there should be no schism in the body, but that the members should have the same care for one another. And if one member suffers, all the members suffer with it; or if one member is honored all the members rejoice with it. (1 Cor. 12:14–26)

Now you are the body of Christ and members individually. (1 Cor. 12:27)

And God has appointed these in the church: first apostles, second prophets, third teachers, after that miracles, then gifts of healings, helps, administrations, varieties of tongues. (1 Cor. 12:28)

Are all apostles? Are all prophets? Are all teachers? Are all workers of miracles? Do all have gifts of healings? Do all speak with tongues? Do all interpret? But earnestly desire the best gifts. And yet I show you a more excellent way. (1 Cor. 12:29–31)

And He Himself gave some to be apostles, some prophets, some evangelists, and some pastors and teachers. (Eph. 4:11)

For the equipping of the saints for the work of ministry, for the edifying of the body of Christ, till we all come to the unity of the faith and of the knowledge of the son of God, to a perfect man, to the measure of the stature of the fullness of Christ. (Eph. 4:12–13)

That we should no longer be children tossed to and fro, and carried about with every wind of doctrine, by the trickery of men, and in the cunning craftiness of deceitful plotting, but speaking the truth in love may grow up in all things into Him who is the head—Christ—. (Eph. 4:14–15)

But you have not so learned Christ. If indeed you have heard Him and have been taught by Him as the truth is in Jesus. That you put off concerning your former conduct the old man which grows corrupt according to the deceitful lusts and be renewed in the spirit of your mind. And that you put on the new man which was created according to God in true righteousness and holiness. (Eph. 4:20–24)

For through Him we both have access by one Spirit to the Father. (Eph. 2:18)

Now to Him who is able to do exceedingly abundantly above all that we ask or think according to the power that works in us. (Eph. 3:20)

To Him be glory in the church by Christ Jesus to all generations for ever and ever Amen. (Eph. 3:21)

Discussion of Scriptures for Preparation

Aren't those scriptures glorious? Jesus wants us to acknowledge and understand that He has given us spiritual gifts, and it's up to us to nurture them and development them under His guidance and love.

While I can't discuss all of the scriptures in the section above, there are two scriptures that stand out to me: Romans 12:6–8 and 1 Corinthians 12:8–10. These scriptures referred to the spiritual gifts. Romans 12:6–8 speaks to seven spiritual gifts. 1 Corinthians 12:8–10 speaks to nine spiritual gifts. As I read these scriptures, I reminded myself that my spiritual gifts are irrevocable. My spiritual gifts are with me forever. I have a responsibility to serve God's people for life. What awesome shoes to wear! Can I fit them? I pray every day for you, Jesus, to give me the strength to answer your call, your assignments that you have bestowed upon me. One of them was writing this book.

Which scriptures are significant to you and your personal experiences? Take a few minutes and reflect on how the scriptures relate in your life. Did a scripture stand out and resonate from within?

Lesson 1: Preparation

Reading and meditating on the scriptures is one thing (I do it every day), but to put it into practice and share the word is what Jesus wants. In the next section, I share excerpts from my memoirs before my prayer group meeting, which takes place once a week on Fridays from seven p.m. to nine p.m. As you'll see, before I even understood the Spiritual Wheel of GOD, Jesus was giving me guidance, and I was asking Him questions on how to handle His instructions for that night.

I read the scriptures right after my morning prayers, and I read them again after I got back from my colleague's funeral. After I finished reading the scriptures for the third time (I had read them the night before), I'd asked Jesus about the prayer meeting that was scheduled later that evening.

November 8, 2013
Friday morning prayers

"Good morning, dear Jesus. May I ask you a question?"

Yes, My child.

"Are you going to give me instructions before I go to the prayer meeting tonight, or are you going to wait and give me instructions step by step as we go?"

I will give you instructions as we go. You will speak to the group and start off by saying, "Jesus has asked me to give an example of the supernatural experience that took place before I started my ministry among the people with my spiritual gifts." You will give your testimony. You will explain that you are sharing your story because there are people in this room who will begin to receive their spiritual gifts from Jesus. You will ask the co-prayer leader to lead the Alleluia song for those who will receive the gift of tongues. You will tell them that two prayer members will receive their gifts tonight. A prayer member and the man who is seeing apparitions will receive the gift of tongues. The other prayer members will be amazed at what they will see tonight. During prayers, you will give messages to several people. You will give the testimony of the swinging of your spirit on the ceiling.

Do not worry. I will take you step by step. You will be pleased with the results of tonight. You will have lots to talk about for your book including this meeting between us right now. Do not worry. Everything will work out great.

You will leave soon. Relax before you go. Everything will work out fine.

November 8, 2013
Friday evening prayer group meeting

I was prepared for the prayer meeting that night. Jesus gave me an overview of what was to take place. I knew the two people who would get the gift of tongues. I went at my usual time. I was there in time to continue singing praises to our Lord Jesus. I loved going because I could feel the presence of the Lord among us. "For where two or three are gathered together in my name, there am I in the mist of them" (Matt. 18:20).

I went inside and they were singing and praising the Lord. We then went around and greeted one another. We sat down and it was time to give our testimonies of what the Lord has done for us. As everyone went around to give their testimonies, I realized I would have a testimony to share. Usually I don't say much, but after hearing Jesus' instructions, I had plenty to say!

Suddenly, I began to get nervous. I was so strong before the prayer meeting, but all eyes were on me. Earlier in the meeting, I had told the children in our prayer group to "feel their fear and say it anyway." Now it was time to live by my own words.

My face grew hot, and my throat felt dry, but I had to do this. "I have a testimony," I said in a shaky voice. I told the group that I was a little nervous, so I asked the group to first pray over me so that I could hear Jesus speaking to me, and they did. When they finished, I told them what Jesus told me. "The Lord will start giving the members their spiritual gifts," I said.

Everyone smiled. Courage filled me to continue. "Jesus said your gifts are irrevocable, and for you to use your gifts wisely. Jesus wants you to know that when you first begin to use your gifts, evil will attack you and try to put fear into you." They stared at me with wide eyes. *It's now or never,* I thought to myself. So, I shared my testimony of when evil snatched my spirit out of my body.

My Testimony

On the night of November 13, 2009, I was lying in bed reading before going to sleep for the night. When I finished reading, I turned off my lamp on the nightstand and lay on my back. Suddenly, before I could barely put my head on the pillow, something snatched me out of my body and was swinging my spirit around at the top of the ceiling. As I was going around and around, I thought, *Help! What is going on?*

I was stunned, and dizzy, and shocked, and I had no idea what was happening. In a steady voice, I said, "I rebuke you in the name of Jesus." But I kept going around and around at the top of the ceiling. And then I shouted with conviction, "I REBUKE YOU IN THE NAME OF JESUS!"

I dropped back down into my body like a slippery, wet, cooked spaghetti. I immediately sat up in the bed, turned on the light, and said, "What was that?" I wasn't dreaming because I had just lay down and hadn't gone to sleep yet. I was nervous because I didn't understand what had happened.

At the end of the week, I went to my sister and brother-in-law's church. I spoke to my brother-in-law, who is a minister in another Christian denomination about what had happened to me. "It was the devil," my brother-in-law said. My heart dropped. "Jesus must have something very special for you to do," he said. Before he became a pastor, he, too, had an encounter with the devil. He was going to tell me about it, but a church member came over to ask a question.

Well, I felt better after talking to him because at least I knew I wasn't crazy. What I now know is that something may happen just before you start receiving your gifts and are getting ready to do your ministry for God.

The experience of being snatched out of my body happened during the time I was taking a nine-week seminar with my church. After the experience of being snatched out of my body, I began to hear Jesus clearly speaking to me in my morning prayers, as if He were having a conversation with me. I heard Him through my thoughts, word for word, daily and consistently. He would give me assignments, and I knew exactly what to do. I heard Him before, but not like this. It was awesome! I could feel His holiness as the thoughts came to me. I also received the gift of tongues during that seminar.

I shared this story with my prayer group that night. I told them that Jesus would give spiritual gifts to them. I also shared that two people would receive the gift of tongues that night. Jesus told me that the co-prayer leader would lead the Alleluia song. I then turned to the co-prayer leader and said, "You can proceed."

Silence came over the room. The co-prayer leader looked a little stunned. She then talked about how the Lord delivered a message to her that morning that He was going to start giving the charismatic gifts to prayer members, but He didn't tell her anything about leading an Alleluia song. Hesitantly, she explained how the Alleluia song worked. You sing "alleluia" repeatedly, and some people may begin to speak tongues. There were a few new people in the meeting that night, so she wanted to make sure everyone understood what to do.

The room is set up with comfortable chairs arranged in a circle, so we are all facing each other. When we stand up, we are already in a circle to sing. We stood up as the co-prayer leader led us in singing alleluia.

As we were singing the song, Jesus had me to go to the center of the circle and walk over to a prayer member to pray tongues over her. I then went back to my place. A little while later, Jesus instructed me to go to the center again, and I walked over to another prayer member. As I was praying tongues over her, a member next to her started making sounds in front of everyone. She then flopped down as if overwhelmed with emotions. She eventually got up and joined the group again in singing alleluia. The co-prayer leader ended the singing, and everyone sat back down again.

Jesus had told me that a prayer member would be asked to give a presentation from the Bible. The member would select a scripture they would like to discuss. The topic selected was on faith. After the presentation, there was an interesting discovery! There was a mother-daughter duo present, and the mother had given the presentation. After she was finished, the daughter said, "I opened to the same scripture this morning!" The mother and daughter did not know until the prayer meeting that they had read the same scripture.

It is amazing how God works! It was very appropriate to discuss faith, which tied into needing faith to accept the spiritual gifts that Jesus had for the group.

November 9, 2013
Saturday morning prayers

You did a good job last night, Dr. Jacquie. ["Dr. Jacquie" is the spiritual name Jesus gave me.] *Even if members decide not to come, you will continue with the lesson. Even if people will not do what they are supposed to do, you just worry about the message. You do not interpret the message. It is up to them to decide what to do with the messages. They can ask a question, and I will tell them what to do with the message or give further clarification.*

A prayer member will come back at the next meeting and tell the group they know how to speak tongues. Their faith will determine when they receive it. One prayer member received hers in the prayer meeting. Another will receive hers on Sunday in church. Another member received the gift of healing. He has already told the prayer leader and the co-prayer leader.

You have lots more work to do. You will be very pleased with it all.

You will document what took place at the prayer meeting last night. You will document each lesson. You will see the outcome of the book and will show how things happen and sometimes things didn't happen. You will tell them that people have free will and can determine the outcome by their participation or with non-participation. It is done unto you as you believe [Matt. 9:29.]

You are helping the prayer members. They are happy that you are there, and you are showing how things work with Life in the Spirit. The co-prayer leader will be given the message about each lesson as we go. It is not for them to decide how you deliver the message.

The member who was seated at your right wants to talk to you. Some strange things have happened to her. The members who are having strange things happen to them will ask you questions to help them, and you will help them. They will be very pleased with it all.

Your reputation is growing among the members of the church. A prayer member will bring people with her to the prayer meetings. The prayer meeting is growing. It will get bigger and bigger. The co-prayer leader knows what is happening and she loves it. She knows what is happening with you. She knows you are a very holy person who is very obedient to the Lord. She was very pleased with it all. She is going to call you during the week, and she is going to encourage you to do God's work in the prayer meetings.

[The co-prayer leader never called during that time.]

A prayer member is going to be instructed to go to you. She is going to call you to bring you up to date with what is going on in the house. I will tell you what to do and say.

[A prayer member did not call me at that time.]

You have arrived. You will be reported to a charismatic priest and the parish priest from the church about last night's prayer meeting. Someone will approach you next Friday. They will want to ask you questions. The charismatic priest will want to ask you some questions. He already knows he will be working with you. He will tell you so next Friday. Do not worry. You will be pleased.

[The priest did not contact me.]

November 10, 2013
Sunday morning prayers

You are so obedient. You did not let the prayer leader intimidate you. You were nervous, and you prayed for My help. You knew how to overcome him, and it will work every time. Pray to me, Jesus Christ. Remember, I am with you 24/7. You will be very pleased with it all.

I received many messages from Jesus at that time, and I was especially grateful that He chose me to tell my church members about the spiritual gifts. Yes, I was nervous. As I mentioned before, I tend to keep quiet at prayer group, but I couldn't stay quiet that weekend. Jesus had given me a task, and I couldn't disappoint Him!

We need to prepare ourselves for how we are to embark on receiving the spiritual gifts. We have to be able to accept responsibility to serve God's people. There will be times when you may not want to do or perform the assignments given to you by Jesus. You may be frightened from lack of courage, or maybe you're just tired of serving. I have to remind myself that the anointing is a lifetime commitment, and Jesus will see me through any obstacles that may get in my way. We must keep going and keep serving God's people according to our purpose and ministry God has given us.

To better help us understand *preparation*, the first lesson of the Spiritual Wheel of GOD, God has provided seven key points to remember.

The Seven Keys for Preparation

Lesson 1, "Preparation," helps us to get ready to take on the responsibilities of obtaining spiritual gifts and to perform the assignments as given. The seven keys help us to understand the responsibility that goes along with Preparation.

The seven keys for Lesson 1 are *the Holy Spirit, your spirit, humility, criticism, fasting, discipline,* and *surrendering.*

1. **Holy Spirit**: Learn how to hear the Holy Spirit.
2. **Your Spirit**: Learn how to prepare your spirit for the spiritual gift.
3. **Humility**: Learn how to be humble. It is not you, but the Father above. Jesus Christ does all the work.
4. **Criticism**: Be open to criticism. Not everyone will believe or even accept that you have a spiritual gift(s).

5. **Fasting**: Learn how to fast and do prayer before using your spiritual gift(s).
6. **Discipline:** Be disciplined, self-controlled, and competent.
7. **Surrendering:** Learn how to surrender yourself to be ready to give up everything to follow Jesus.

Key 1: The Holy Spirit

You must learn how to live in the spirit to hear the Holy Spirit so you will be able to be led by the Holy Spirit. You must hear the Holy Spirit to receive your gifts and to know what to do with them. For it is the Holy Spirit that does all the work. You listen and you obey what He tells you to do. You must hear Him to serve God's people. You must hear Him to know what to do. How else will you be able to be obedient if you do not know what to do? It is not your desire to serve God's people the way you want to serve them. It is God's desire. You will be pleased with the desires of God's heart.

> If we live in the Spirit, let us also follow the Spirit. (Gal. 5:25)

As each one has received a gift, use it to serve one another as good stewards of God's varied grace. Whoever preaches, let it be with the words of God; whoever serves, let it be with the strength that God supplies, so that in all things God may be glorified through Jesus Christ, to whom belong glory and dominion forever and ever. Amen. (1 Peter 4:10–11.)

Key 2: Your Spirit

You must learn how to prepare your spirit for the spiritual gift(s). You will need to pray for God to give you your spiritual gift. You must be open to God's words. If you cannot hear the Holy Spirit on a regular basis every day, you will need to prepare your spirit to hear Him.

> To hear God's voice, we must belong to God. Jesus said, "My sheep hear me; I know them, and they follow me. I give them eternal life, and they shall never perish. No one can take them out of my hand." (John 10:27–28.)

The Listening Prayer

Listening to the Lord is very special. You must focus and learn how to concentrate on the Word. It is through the Word that you learn how to communicate with Jesus every day. Jesus will tell you things that will help you grow spiritually for the good of His people. You must have patience when you are learning how to hear Him. It is like learning how to ride a bike. You will not learn how to ride a bike in one day. To ride it well, it may take a week or more depending on how much time you spend practicing. It is the same way with listening to the Holy Spirit. You must practice. I have found a routine that works for me, but it took a lot of trial and error. I practice what I call the Listening Prayer. In order to hear the Holy Spirit, I need the environment to be quiet. That is why I sit up in bed when I wake up in the morning when my mind is alert. Then I get my laptop that is next to the bed. I sit quietly in bed and breathe slowly in and out as I wait for Jesus to speak to me.

Here are a few tips on how you can go about your own practice of hearing and listening to the Holy Spirit. Keep in mind that everyone is different and will have a different process.

Practicing the Listening Prayer

- Find a quiet time and place without disturbance that you will be able to repeat every day.
- Sit quietly with a pen and journal or a laptop, whichever you feel comfortable using.
- Begin your Listening Prayer by asking the Holy Spirit to speak to you.
- Wait to hear His Word.
- In the beginning, you will have to learn how to focus and not let thoughts come into your mind. Renounce the thoughts away.
- Listen for the Holy Spirit to speak as though you are trying to hear someone whisper something in your ear.
- Learn where to find that quiet place where you can hear the Holy Spirit.
- As you begin to hear the Holy Spirit—either through sound or thought—write down His words in your journal.

- Do not try to understand what is being said, just write it, and after the Holy Spirit has finished speaking to you, you will then read your journal for understanding.
- Should you need clarity as you read, ask the Holy Spirit your question and then wait to listen to what He has to say.

You will learn how to communicate with the Holy Spirit to the point that you will be able to ask questions and receive answers any time of the day 24/7. You determine through free will how much you are willing to put into learning how to listen to the Holy Spirit through the Listening Prayer.

Spiritual Freedom Check Meditation

Just like you listen to the Holy Spirit every day through the Listening Prayer, you should also prepare your mind to receive information from the Holy Spirit. I like to do a Spiritual Freedom Check meditation. This type of meditation keeps the evil spirits away—they try to keep us trapped and spiritually in bondage through negative emotions. To help set yourself free from evil and negative emotions, you will need to do a spiritual meditation daily. Just like you brush your teeth every day for gum and teeth health, as well as full-body health, you need to do the same thing for your spirit by keeping your mind strong and healthy. Spiritual Freedom Check meditations help us to get rid of evil thoughts and spirits.

> For you were called for freedom, brothers. But do not use this freedom as an opportunity for the flesh; rather, serve one another through love. (Galatians 5:13)

November 11, 2017
Saturday morning prayers

"Jesus, why do I need to do Spiritual Freedom Check Meditations?"

Spiritual freedom checks are a way to have good maintenance in your mind to keep the negative triggers from past experiences away, and to practice keeping the soul swept out and cleaned of negative thought debris. When you allow negative thoughts to build up, things begin to get out of hand.

When you are with a negative evil spirit, you do negative evil things. When you are in a loving and kind spirit, you will do loving and kind things.

Do your Spiritual Freedom Check meditation in the mornings. You will feel better throughout the day. Freedom checks can at times be like a Band-Aid to protect the sore until it heals. Like a Band-Aid has its place for healing, so does the Spiritual Freedom Check Meditation.

Every day, preferably in the morning before you go out to start your day, you can go through your Spiritual Freedom Check meditation. You can do it as often as you need it. Sometimes things happen during the day that would warrant a Spiritual Freedom Check meditation to get you back on board to your spiritual freedom.

If you are not able to get rid of negative emotions, you may have to dig deeper to find the root of your negative feelings. For example, someone who is depressed and really can't shake that feeling away even with a spiritual meditation will need to use other instruments to help them. That person may need help getting to the root of why he or she feels depressed and getting to the root is getting to the truth of what is going on. Pray and ask the Lord to give you the information you need to know to get to the root of your problem even if it means you may need professional counseling.

The Five Steps of the Spiritual Freedom Check Meditation

The Spiritual Freedom Check Meditation includes five steps: preparation, identify evil spirits, renounce evil spirits, command evil spirits to be gone, and ask the Lord to keep you in His Kingdom with your true spiritual identity, purpose, and ministry/destiny.

Step 1: Preparation

In order to perform this meditation, you will need to find a quiet place where you won't be interrupted or distracted. I like to sit quietly in a chair in my room with my hands on my lap with my palms up listening for any thoughts from the Lord. Relax your body. Drop your shoulders if you feel tension in them.

Take a deep breath slowly through your nose. Hold it for a few seconds and then exhale slowly through your mouth.

To start your meditation, consider saying something that is meaningful to your current situation. I like to get in tune with my emotions. I look for negative vibes of any kind. Here is an example of what you could say:

> *Good morning, dear Jesus. I want to do my Spiritual Freedom Check meditation this morning. I so humbly ask you to help me recognize any emotion(s) I might have that is tied to an evil spirit(s) that I need to get rid of.*

After you ask the Lord to help you, pause for a moment and wait to see if He gives you an answer. If He responds, you will write whatever He says in your journal.

Step 2: Identify Negative Emotions

Ask yourself, "How am I feeling right now in this very moment? Do I feel angry, sad, scared? Do negative thoughts keep coming to mind? Or am I happy, joyful, appreciative, humbled?" Remember, you can have both positive and negative emotions.

Now turn your focus to the negative emotions that will hinder you from your spiritual freedom for the day. It can be more than one. It could be several, depending on your feelings. For example, if you're feeling sad, acknowledge that you're feeling sad. Then question why you are feeling sad and identify the source. Maybe it's because you went through some old photographs while you were cleaning and felt nostalgic for a happier time.

Once you have identified the negative feelings, you will be able to, in the name of Jesus Christ, renounce the negative feelings away by their evil-spiritual names. Those evil feelings are evil spirits. Evil spirits can influence how you feel and behave throughout the day. For example, maybe you feel angry after having a fight with your spouse, and that anger will linger and bleed into other areas of your life. Maybe you are driving, and someone cuts you off and you shout at that person. Or maybe you snap at your coworker over something trivial. When we let our negative emotions linger in our lives without attempting to deal with them or face them, they will cloud our minds and our spirit.

Step 3: Renounce Evil Spirits

You will renounce the evil spirit(s). While we may not think of "sadness" or "depression" as being "evil," per se, these emotions can hinder how we live our lives. Depression, for example, is often fueled by negative thoughts, thus thinking, and bringing up negative thoughts can lead to depression. There are various degrees of depression that can range from sad feelings to despair and hopelessness. These negative thoughts can be identified in the Spiritual Freedom Check Meditation as well as depression itself.

You will say, "In the name of Jesus Christ, I renounce the evil spirit (name the evil spirit)."

Step 4: "In the name of Jesus Christ, I command the evil Spirits (name the evil spirits) to Leave."

I like to take a few more breaths to center myself. Check for any other negative emotions that may be present. Look for signs of evil from within. Maybe you still have anger brewing from that fight with your spouse. It's time to let it go. You will command the evil spirits in the name of Jesus Christ to leave.

You will say, "With the authority in me in the Name of Jesus Christ, I command [name the evil spirits] to leave now and permanently never to return."

You may have to do this a few times. You may be surprised how many emotions are swirling around in your head!

Step 5: Ask the Lord for Help

You will ask the Lord to keep you in His Kingdom.
You will say, "I ask you Lord to keep me in Your Kingdom with my true identity, purpose, ministry, and destiny."

The Spiritual Freedom Check Meditation helps your mind and spirit stay free and open and healthy. I would recommend doing this spiritual meditation daily.

Key 3: Humility

After serving God's people as His vessel, Jesus Christ would often tell me to say, "It is not I, but the Father above. It is Jesus Christ who does all the work."

Do not let the devil fool you into thinking that you are doing it and allow your ego to get in the way of the Lord's work. You do not have time for that. God's work is too important to get caught up doing His work on your time or trying to modify something that God has told you to do.

I am so grateful that the Lord has chosen me to help save souls. I am aware that I am just His vessel and that He does all the work. I oftentimes just thank the Lord for bestowing His grace upon me. I am honored to be a soldier of the Lord. I am honored to write His book as His vessel. I know my thoughts to write this book came from the Lord. Thank you, Jesus, thank you.

> Let every soul be subject to the governing authorities. For there is no authority except from God, and authorities that exist are appointed by God. (Rom. 13:1)

Do not be so foolish to think that you can perform the miracles yourself. You are a vessel that God uses to do His work. Be humble to know that it is God's authority that does all the work, not you. Do not let the earthly side have you thinking that you yourself are doing it.

> Let us not be conceited, provoking one another, envious of one another. (Gal. 5:26)

Be humble. Don't be jealous or want someone else's anointing but seek your anointing from God through prayer. Let God's will be done.

Key 4: Criticism

Be open to criticism. Everyone will not believe or even accept that you do in fact have spiritual gifts.

> If possible, on your part, live at peace with all. (Rom 12:18)

You must have faith in yourself that you can perform your spiritual gift(s) and that you know you have the gift. Evil will try to cast doubt and put confusion in you if you let it. You must have faith that you can perform the gifts and do what God has given you.

Do not worry about what others think of you and your gifts. You only must worry about what God thinks of you. None of the people around you will be there with you come Judgement Day. You will be judged by God and God alone. The Lord will guide you through your journey with your spiritual gifts. Listen to the Holy Spirit and do as you are told. Be obedient to the Lord and you will be rewarded for it.

Constructive criticism is good for you. Many times, the criticism you will receive may be of people doubting that you have a spiritual gift. It is not for them to judge you, but for the Lord. Keep going regardless of what people might say or think of you.

Key 5: Fasting

You will need to prepare yourself to perform the holy gifts. The spiritual gifts—*wisdom, knowledge, faith, healing, mighty deeds, prophecy, discernment, tongues*, and *interpretation of tongues* (1 Cor. 12:8–10)—are holy gifts and should be treated as such. You need to do a cleansing of the mind and soul. Fasting will help strengthen your ability to perform the spiritual task before you. You need to pray for forgiveness, and to pray for good health to perform and deliver the assignments presented before you. You must learn how to fast. Know what it means to fast. Certain miracles can only be performed through fasting and prayer.

Fasting and prayer are often linked together in the Bible.

> . . . and then as a widow until she was eighty-four. She never left the temple, but worshiped night and day with fasting and prayer. (Luke 2:37)

> While they were worshiping the Lord and fasting, the Holy Spirit said' "Set apart for me Barnabas and Saul for the work to which I have called them." Then completing their fasting and prayer, they laid hands on them and sent them on their way. (Acts 13:2–3)

Fasting is a way to demonstrate to God and ourselves that we are serious about our relationship with Him and our anointing that He has bestowed upon us. Fasting and prayer helps you to remove yourself from the worldly things and to focus on God and what He has in store for you as your identity and destiny in this world during this lifetime.

Fasting should be set for a period of time, especially when fasting from food. But there are other ways to fast with prayers. In 1 Corinthians 7:5, the Bible says, "Do not deprive each other, except perhaps by mutual consent for a time, to be free for prayer, but then return to one another, so Satan may not tempt you through your lack of self-control."

> Moreover, when you fast, do not be like the hypocrites, with a sad countenance. For they disfigure their faces that they may appear to men to be fasting. Assuredly, I say to you, they have their reward. But you, when you fast, anoint your head and wash your face, so that you do not appear to men to be fasting, but to your Father who

> is in the secret place; and your Father who sees in secret will reward you openly. (Matt. 6:16–18)

Key 6: Discipline

As with anything, it's important to have discipline and be able to control your actions, emotions, and reactions. When you are preparing to receive spiritual gifts, you must be able to have a strong handle on discipline that encompasses self-control and competency.

> Therefore, I run in such a way, as not without aim; I box in such a way, as not beating the air. But I discipline my body and make it my slave, so that, after I have preached to others, I myself will not be disqualified. (1 Cor. 9:26–27)

You must be ready to listen to the Holy Spirit every day. You need to allow the Lord to lead your life. You should have a special time and place every day to listen to the Holy Spirit.

It will take discipline and self-control to do it on a consistent basis. You need discipline to hear the Holy Spirit. You need discipline to do what the Holy Spirit tells you to do. You must have discipline to do what you are told even when you do not feel like doing it or do not have the courage to do it. If you feel afraid, be obedient and do it anyway. It will take hard work to do God's work. You must have the discipline to be consistent in what you are told to do and to perform your spiritual gifts.

> For God did not give us a spirit of cowardice but rather of power and love and self-control. (2 Tim. 1:7)
>
> All scripture is inspired by God and is useful for teaching, for refutation, for correction, and for training in righteousness, so that one who belongs to God may be competent, equipped for every good work. (2 Tim. 3:16–17)
>
> In contrast, the fruit of the Spirit is love, joy, peace, patience, kindness, generosity, faithfulness, gentleness, and self-control. Against such there is no law. Now those who belong to Christ [Jesus] have crucified their flesh with its passions and desires. If we live in the Spirit, let us also follow the Spirit. (Gal. 5:22–25)

Key 7: Surrendering

When you receive your spiritual gift, you must be ready to be obedient and go where Jesus leads you even if it means doing things differently from what you are used to doing, going to places you are used to going, or even how you live your life. The concept of "surrendering" is hard for people to understand. It takes a lot of faith and discipline to surrender. The key to all of this is surrendering. Surrender yourself. Be ready to give up everything to follow Jesus.

> Then Jesus said to his disciples, "Whoever wishes to come after me must deny himself, take up his cross, and follow me. For whoever wishes to save his life will lose it, but whoever loses his life for my sake will find it." (Matt. 16:24–25)

Summary

Lesson 1, "Preparation," is the first spoke in the Spiritual Wheel of GOD (the Gifts of Development). Preparation will be helpful prior to receiving your spiritual gift(s) (wisdom, knowledge, faith, healing, mighty deeds, prophecy, discernment, tongues, and interpretation of tongues, 1 Cor. 12:8–10). Some may receive one gift, and others may receive more than one spiritual gifts.

The seven keys in Lesson 1 are: *The Holy Spirit, your spirit, humility, criticism, fasting, discipline, and surrendering.*

You need to learn how to hear the Holy Spirit so that you can receive your assignments that God has specifically for you. You will learn how to prepare your spirit for the spiritual gifts.

You must learn how to be humble and know it is not you but the Father above and Jesus Christ who does all the work. You are just a vessel that God uses. The power comes from God. In doing God's work, you must also be open to criticism. Everyone will not believe or even accept that you have spiritual gifts.

You must prepare yourselves through fasting and prayer before even using your gifts. It will take discipline, self-control, and competence to perform your spiritual gifts. The most important thing you need to know in preparing yourself for your ministry is to be ready to give up everything to follow Jesus. Are you committed? Are you ready to give up everything to follow Jesus?

Chapter 2
Lesson 2: People

"As each one has received a gift, use it to serve one another as good stewards of God's varied grace." ~ *1 Peter 4:10*

Your spiritual gifts are for God's people not for you. You minister to others and others minister to you.

The second spoke in the Spiritual Wheel of GOD is "People." The second spoke is to focus on your gift in serving God's people.

In Lesson 2, I present the scriptures that were given to me by my prayer partner in the order given to me. I discuss my experience of presenting Lesson 2 to my Charismatic prayer group, as well as my testimony of when I accidentally locked my keys in the trunk of my car. Finally, I discuss the seven keys that will help you understand your responsibility in serving God's people.

The scriptures in this lesson focus on you, the people, and to understand who you are. There is a spirit of God and a spirit of the world. They are different and are governed differently. God dwells in you. You receive and are taught by the Spirit of God, and you will have eternal life with Him. Though you are taught by the Spirit, you are still in the world as humans (flesh), and you behave in ordinary human ways. Humans who can become believers in God are led by Jesus Christ through the Holy Spirit.

Scriptures for People

> . . . this God has revealed to us through the Spirit. For the Spirit scrutinizes everything, even the depths of God. Among human beings, who knows what pertains to a person except the spirit of the person that is within? Similarly, no one knows what pertains to God except the Spirit of God. We have not received the spirit of the world but the Spirit that is from God, so that we understand the things freely given us by God. And we speak about them not with words taught by human wisdom, but with words taught by the Spirit, describing spiritual terms. (1 Cor. 2:10–13)
>
> Now the natural person does not accept what pertains to the Spirit of God, for to him it is foolishness, and he cannot understand it, because it is judged spiritually.

The spiritual person, however, can judge everything but is not subject to judgment by anyone. (1 Cor. 2:14–15)

For "who has known the mind of the Lord, so as to counsel him?" But we have the mind of Christ. (1 Cor. 2:16)

Do you not know that you are the temple of God, and that the Spirit of God dwells in you? If anyone destroys God's temple, God will destroy that person; for the temple of God, which you are, is holy. (1 Cor. 3:16–17)

But as it is written: "What eye has not seen, and ear has not heard, and what has not entered the human heart, what God has prepared for those who love him." (1 Cor. 2:9)

. . . and again. "The Lord knows the thoughts of the wise, that they are vain." (1 Cor. 3:20)

Paul or Apollos or Cephas, or the world or life or death, or the present, or the future: all belong to you, (1 Cor. 3:22)

. . . and you to Christ, and Christ to God. (1 Cor. 3:23)

. . . for you are still of the flesh. While there is jealousy and rivalry among you, are you not of the flesh, and behaving in an ordinary human way? (1 Cor. 3:3)

Whenever someone says, "I belong to Paul" and another, "I belong to Apollos," are you not merely human? What is Apollos, after all, and what is Paul? Ministers through whom you became believers, just as the Lord assigned each one. (1 Cor. 3:4–5)

I planted, Apollos watered, but God caused the growth. (1 Cor. 3:6)

Therefore, neither the one who plants nor the one who waters are anything, but only God, who causes the growth. The one who plants and the one who waters are equal, and each will receive wages in proportion to his labor. For we are God's co-workers; you are God's field, God's building. (1 Cor. 3:7–9)

According to the grace of God given to me, like a wise master builder I laid a foundation, and another is building upon it. But each one must be careful how he builds upon it, for no one can lay a foundation other than the one that is there, namely Jesus Christ. (1 Cor. 3:10–11)

> Now it is of course required of stewards that they be found trustworthy. (1 Cor. 4:2)
>
> I have applied these things to myself and Apollos for your benefit, brothers, so that you may learn from us not to go beyond what is written, so that none of you will be inflated with pride in favor of one person over against another. (1 Cor. 4:6)
>
> Who confers distinction upon you? What do you possess that you have not received? But if you have received it, why are you boasting as if you did not receive it? (1 Cor. 4:7)
>
> Do you not know that your body is a temple of the Holy spirit within you, whom you have from God, and that you are not your own? for you have been purchased at a price. Therefore, glorify God in your body. (1 Cor. 6:19–20)
>
> He must increase; I must decrease. (John 3:30)
>
> Whoever does accept his testimony certifies that God is trustworthy. For the one whom God sent speaks the words of God. He does not ration his gift of the Spirit. The Father loves the Son and has given everything over to him. (John 3:33–35)
>
> Whoever believes in the son has eternal life, but whoever disobeys the Son will not see life, but the wrath of God remains upon him. (John 3:36)
>
> John answered and said, "No one can receive anything except what has been given him from Heaven." (John 3:27)

Discussion of Scriptures for People

While I can't discuss all of the scriptures in this section, I want to point out a few that resonated with me: 1 Corinthians 2:10, John 3:33–36, and 1 Corinthians 3:16. In order to help God's people, I must know who I am and clearly who I serve. I must be able to distinguish between the spirit of God who lives in me and the spirit of the world that I live in. We have a part of God within us as the temple of the Holy Spirit. I am pleased that I have spiritual gifts. I pray that I receive all the spiritual gifts the Holy Spirit has for me in order to serve His people.

Which scriptures are significant to you and your personal experiences? Take a few minutes and reflect on how the scriptures relate in your life, if at all. Did a scripture stand out and resonate from within?

Lesson 2: People

In this section, I provide excerpts of my memoirs of my conversations with Jesus in my morning prayers. We did not have a prayer meeting on Friday, November 15, 2013, but Jesus spoke to me anyway on Monday, November 11, 2013. He also spoke to me on November 22, 2013.

November 11, 2013
Monday morning prayers

The scriptures your prayer partner gave you are for Lesson 2. The next time you go to the prayer meeting, you will give another testimony. This testimony will be about your experience when you locked your keys in the trunk of your car. Your testimony will be used to explain to those who think that they are performing their gifts themselves rather than being a vessel for Jesus. They need to understand when they receive the gift that they are not using the gift—Jesus is doing it. It will only be done through the will of God. Messages can come from anyone. You will know when a message is for you. If you have doubt, pray, and ask God to reveal or confirm His answer to you. This lesson is for several in the room who have gifts and now think they are performing their gift themselves. You will help them to understand. They will ask you questions. You will be able to answer any question that comes your way.

November 22, 2013
Friday morning prayers

You have a lesson to give tonight. You will read over your scriptures. You will give the testimony of when you locked your keys in the trunk. It was the night you learned your special gifts are not for you but to give to God's people. It is a ministry for the people. You minister to others and others minister to you. You can always receive messages from people who may not even know they are giving a message, but you will know when you receive the message. I will guide you through it. You will know what to say in the same way a minister preaches their sermon. They just know what to say.

November 22, 2013
Friday evening prayer group meeting

On that Friday night at prayer meeting, I discussed my testimony of how I learned the lesson that my spiritual gifts are to serve God's people. Believe it or not, I learned this lesson because I had locked my keys in the trunk of my car!

I prepared for the prayer meeting for the night. I read the scriptures and meditated on what Jesus wanted me to talk about for the lesson. There were fewer members at the meeting from the last time. It was the week before Thanksgiving, and it was sort of expected. Part of the prayer group meeting is for sharing what God has done for us in the week prior.

As usual, we sat around in a circle and went around the room to ask what God has done for us. I waited until everyone had spoken. My message was important. Jesus had instructed me to teach the members of my prayer group the second lesson, that our spiritual gifts should serve God's people and not to be used for personal purposes.

I smiled and said, "Thank you for listening to what I have to say." The group nodded and smiled. "I want to share my testimony because Jesus told me to share His word about spiritual gifts." I then explained what had happened that day.

My Testimony

I work at two colleges. I am an associate professor and a lecturer. I lecture at one college during the day and the other college in the evening. I have two keys, one for each classroom. On that day, I had finished my morning class, went home for lunch and to grade some assignments, and then I went to my evening class. I gathered my things and walked across campus to the building where I taught my class. But just before I stepped inside, I noticed that I had my key for my morning class. So, I walked all the way back to my car. I opened the trunk. I quickly searched through a few things and found the bag I use for my morning class, unzipped the front pocket, and pulled out the key. When I slammed the trunk shut, my stomach dropped. *My car keys!* In my haste, I had haphazardly tossed the car keys to the side as I searched for my other key. I could have panicked, but I didn't worry about it. I knew Jesus had given me special gifts so I could easily get the trunk open with prayer.

So, I stepped back from the car and I prayed, asking Jesus to open the trunk. I waited a few minutes and then I walked up to the trunk and attempted to open it, but it would not open. *Maybe I didn't pray right,* I thought. So, I stepped back and tried again. I prayed a little longer, a couple more times, but the trunk wouldn't open. I had to call AAA service and wait for someone to open the trunk. The whole thing took about three hours!

It was an important lesson for me. I think we're all guilty of wanting help in those moments, which is only human. The difference, however, is that we can sometimes feel *entitled* to get help from our Lord. That we *deserve* to have our prayers answered because we are asking for help. But our spiritual gifts are not for us. Our spiritual gifts are to be used as God sees fit.

In that moment with the keys, I realized that the gifts I received from Jesus were not meant for me but for God's people. I realized then that I serve in one plate to God's people, and I eat and receive from another plate. I understand now how things go. It is not me but the Father above who makes things happen. Jesus Christ does all the work. Jesus decides what we can and cannot do. I am just the vessel that He uses to do His work. My spiritual gifts are not for me to use for my own selfish means.

The Seven Keys for People

Lesson 2, "People," discusses how your spiritual gifts are for God's people not for you. The seven keys help us to understand the responsibility that goes along with using our gifts to help God's people.

The seven keys for Lesson 2 are *people, service, difficulties, assistance, persistence, non-judgment,* and *reward.*

1. **People**: Spiritual gifts are for God's people.
2. **Service**: Use your spiritual gifts to serve others not yourself.
3. **Difficulties**: Help God's people whenever you can no matter how difficult it may be.
4. **Assistance**: People are always in need of help. Evil is all around. Serve God's people with your spiritual gifts.
5. **Persistence**: Never give up or stop helping people just because you don't feel like it. You must be strong to serve God's people.
6. **Non-Judgment**: Do not judge God's people while you serve them. It is not for you to judge.
7. **Reward**: You will be rewarded for serving God's people.

Key 1: People

To serve your God, you must serve God's people. You will use your gifts to help save souls. It is part of your destiny. You serve God's people in one plate and you eat from another (receive your blessings). I thought my spiritual gifts were for me when I locked my keys in my car, but they weren't.

> For God so loved the world that he gave his only son, so that everyone who believes in him might not perish but might have eternal life. For God did not send his son into the world to condemn the world, but that the world might be saved through him. (John 3:16–17)
>
> For the son of Man did not come to be served but to serve and to give his life as a ransom for many. (Mark 10:45)
>
> For I was hungry, and you gave me food, I was thirsty, and you gave me drink, I was a stranger and you welcomed me, I was naked, and you clothed me, ill and you cared for me, in prison and you visited me. (Matt. 25:35–36)

Key 2: Service

Our spiritual gifts are for serving God's people, and you cannot think of yourself while serving for God. You must stay focused on what you are doing, and that is serving God's people.

A good example of this is when we expect something in return. In 2010, I wasn't as spiritually knowledgeable as I am today. I attended a church Charismatic spiritual workshop. We broke out into groups by tables of ten. Many who were there had an anointing with spiritual gifts from the Holy Spirit. Some wanted to learn how to receive them.

As we began to share our experiences, a woman came over to the table and with two other women church members. They sat down on each side of her. As we discussed our supernatural experiences, the women raved about how holy and wonderful the woman was, and that she could perform miracles. The woman seemed proud that she was blessed to perform the miracles. The two women talked all about the woman developing her gifts and neglecting their own.

I then chimed in, "It is Jesus Christ who does all the work. Everyone can receive spiritual gifts from the Holy Spirit, who distributes them as He so desires. We are vessels that God uses."
The woman had the two church members following her around for her own edification and joy. Remember, it is not I but the Father above. It is Jesus Christ who does all the work.

> After this the Lord appointed seventy-two others whom he sent ahead of him in pairs to every town and place he intended to visit. He said to them, "The harvest is abundant, but the laborers are few; so, ask the master of the harvest to send out laborers for his harvest. Go on your way; behold I am sending you like lambs among wolves. Carry no money bag, no sack, no sandals; and greet no one along the way, into whatever house you enter, first say, 'Peace to this household.'" (Luke 10:1–5)

Key 3: Difficulties

Help God's people whenever you can no matter how difficult it may be. When Jesus gave me the assignment to cast out demons in three women at the prayer meeting, I had to mustard up the courage to actually do it. I really was afraid to do it, but I managed to do it anyway.

God never said it would be easy. Even Jesus Christ was crucified. You must have the courage to keep going and help God's people with all your heart and might. You will be rewarded for your good deeds.

> "[But] take care not to perform righteous deeds in order that people may see them; otherwise, you will have no recompense from your heavenly Father, when you give alms, do not blow a trumpet before you, as the hypocrites do in the synagogues and in the streets to win the praise of others. Amen, I say to you, they have received their reward. But when you give alms, do not let your left hand know what your right is doing, so that your alms giving may be secret. And your Father who sees in secret will repay you. (Matt. 6:1–4)

Key 4: Assistance

People are always in need of help, but it may be difficult for you to assist them. If someone came up to you and asked you to pray with them—which is not difficult to do—would you do it?

I am an associate professor at a college. I wear a cross openly. One day, I was on my way to class when a student saw my cross and stopped me. "Excuse me, can you pray with me for a few minutes?" the student asked. I was running late, so I questioned whether I should assist the student. What would you do? We do have choices to make. In this case, I stopped and prayed with him for a few minutes.

Serve God's people with your gifts. There are people all around us who need help from the evil one. With your gifts, you will serve God's people. You will help them.

> All scripture is inspired by God and is useful for teaching, for refutation, for correction, and for training in righteousness, so that one who belongs to God may be competent, equipped for every good work. (2 Tim. 3:16–17)

Key 5: Persistence

There will be days when you will not feel like serving God's people. You will need to do it anyway. You have a responsibility to serve God's people when the time is right to serve, not when it is right for your own personal desires and needs. Never give up or stop helping people just because you don't feel like it.

Let's say you have an important meeting. It's raining, you're tired, and you'd much rather stay home in your pajamas and watch a movie. But you need to go to the meeting because someone there is in need of God's help, and you are the one God chose for the task. You don't get to pick and choose which time you will help save souls. Let God's will be done.

> So shall my word be that goes forth from my mouth;
> It shall not return to me empty but shall do what pleases me [the Lord], achieving the end for which I sent it. (Isaiah 55:11)

Key 6: Non-Judgment

Do not judge God's people while you serve them. It is not for us to do. God will be the one to judge His people.

For example, someone confides in you that they are in a relationship with a married person. They know it is wrong and want to break this cycle that they are in. They no longer want to be in that type of relationship. They ask for prayers to help them. What would you do? Sit there in your mind and judge them, thinking, what type of person would do something like that, breaking up a family's home? Or would you pray and recommend counseling without judgment the same way you would want someone not to judge you?

We are to help save souls unconditionally. Who wants to be judged for what they have done and is now sorry and wants forgiveness? Forgiveness heals. In helping to save souls, we are healing God's people. We have all sinned. Maybe some more than others, but we all have sinned.

> Therefore, do not make any judgement before the appointed time, until the Lord comes, for he will bring to light what is hidden in darkness and will manifest the motives of our hearts, and then everyone will receive praise from God. (1 Cor. 4:5)

Key 7: Reward

When you are obedient to the Lord, you will be rewarded for your good deeds. When you are obedient to the Lord in serving His people, you will be given the desires of your heart. Keep steadfast in being obedient and trustworthy. It will take you a long way.

For example, Jesus has rewarded me in so many ways. I can financially take care of myself. I have a teaching career. I own my own place and have a nice car to get me to and from work without worrying about my car breaking down or if I have enough gas to get to my destination. I do not worry how much time I put into my spiritual work in servicing God's people because I know God will take care of me.

> "Behold, I am coming soon. I bring with me the recompense I will give to each according to his deeds." (Rev. 22:12)

Summary

Lesson 2, "People," is the second spoke in the Spiritual Wheel of GOD (the Gifts of Development). We must understand that our spiritual gifts are just that—a gift from God! And we must do what God commands us to do.

The seven keys are *people, service, difficulties, assistance, persistence, non-judgment,* and *reward.*

Your spiritual gifts are for God's people, not for you. You are to help God's people whenever you can no matter how difficult it may seem. God will reward you for your good deeds. People are always in need of help. Evil is all around. You will serve God's people with your gifts. Never give up or stop helping people just because you don't feel like it.

You must be persistent to serve God's people, and while you serve them, do not judge them. It is not for you to judge. You will be rewarded for serving God's people. While we serve God's people, He will determine how we serve them.

Chapter 3
Lesson 3: Distribution

"God added his testimony by signs and wonders, various acts of power, and distribution of the gifts of the Holy Spirit according to his will." ~ Hebrews. 2:4

When I pray every morning, it's a new opportunity for me to nourish my relationship with Jesus. I relish in it! It's something I look forward to. We are all creatures of habit, and my time in the morning with Jesus fills me up and helps me get through my day.

When Jesus told me about the third lesson in the Spiritual Wheel of GOD, it became clear to me that I have a very important role and purpose on this Earth. God makes that known every day.

Distribution is the third spoke in the Spiritual Wheel of GOD. God distributes His spiritual gifts as He so desires.

In Lesson 3, I share the scriptures that my prayer partner gave me in the order that the Holy Spirit gave to her. I also discuss the type of spiritual gifts the Holy Spirit distributes. I share my experiences at my Charismatic prayer group meeting, my testimony of Jesus' messages, and my testimony of healing a colleague's leg. Finally, I discuss the seven keys that will help you understand your responsibility in serving God's people.

Scriptures for Distribution

In the scriptures, Jesus distributes spiritual gifts to His people at His will. "The last may be first, and the first may be last" (Matthew 19:30). He speaks of the love of the Lord and thy neighbor and of kinds of distributions. It goes on to discuss that you will be rewarded for your good deeds, and what you do on Earth will also be known in heaven. The scriptures speak to God who knows all things. That God speaks through you, and all things are possible through God.

> "Again, [Amen,] I say to you, if two of you agree on earth about anything for which they are to pray, it shall be granted to them by my heavenly father. For where two or three are gathered together in my name, there am I in the midst of them." Then Peter approaching asked him, "Lord, if my brother sins against me, how often must I forgive him? As many as seven times?" Jesus answered, "I

say to you, not seven times but seventy-seven times." (Matt. 18:19–22)

But many who are first will be last, and the last will be first. (Matt. 19:30)

Jesus said to them in reply, "Amen, I say to you, if you have faith and do not waver, not only will you do what has been done to the fig tree, but even if you say to this mountain, 'Be lifted up and thrown into the sea,' it will be done. Whatever you ask for in prayer with faith, you will receive." (Matt. 21:21–22)

Thus, the last will be first, and the first will be last." (Matt. 20:16)

I am the God of Abraham, the God of Isaac, and the God of Jacob? He is not the God of the dead but of the living." (Matt. 22:32)

He said to him, "You shall love the Lord, your God, with all your heart, with all your soul, and with all your mind." . . . The second is like it: You shall love your neighbor as yourself. (Matt. 22:37, 39)

"And the king will say to them in reply, 'Amen, I say to you, whatever you did for one of these least brothers of mine, you did for me.'" (Matt. 25:40)

When he came to the other side, to the territory of Gadarenes, two demoniacs who were coming from the tombs met him. They were so savage that no one could travel by that road. They cried out, "What have you to do with us, son of God? Have you come to torment us before the appointed time?" (Matt. 8:28–29)

Cure the sick, raise the dead, cleanse lepers, drive out demons. Without cost you have received; without cost you are to give. (Matt. 10:8)

"Therefore, do not be afraid of them. Nothing is concealed that will not be revealed, nor secret that will not be known. What I say to you in the darkness, speak in the light; what you hear whispered, proclaim on the housetops" (Matt. 10:26–27)

"Everyone that acknowledges me before others I will acknowledge before my heavenly Father. But whoever denies me before others, I will deny before my heavenly Father." (Matt. 10:32–33).

"Whoever receives a prophet will receive a prophet's reward, and whoever receives a righteous man because he is righteous will receive a righteous man's reward." (Matt. 10:41)

"For it will not be you who speak but the Spirit of your Father speaking through you." (Matt 10:20)

"Blessed are your eyes, because they see, and your ears, because they hear. Amen, I say to you, many prophets and righteous people longed to see what you see but not see it, and to hear what you hear but did not hear it." (Matt. 13:16–17)

At once [Jesus] spoke to them, "Take courage, it is I; do not be afraid." (Matt. 14:27)

"And so, I say to you, 'you are Peter, and upon this rock I will build my church, and the gates of the netherworld shall not prevail against it. I will give you the keys to the kingdom of heaven. Whatever you bind on earth shall be bound in heaven; and whatever you lose on earth shall be loosed in heaven.'" (Matt 16:18–19)

Jesus looked at them and said, "For human beings this is impossible, but for God all things are possible." (Matt. 19:26)

Discussion of Scriptures for Distribution

God loves us. We are special, and He speaks through us and He is with us, as shown in Matthew 18:20, 10:8, and 10:17.
Just to know that when two or three gathers in His name, Jesus will be among us. How holy is that? The Lord is with us even when we pray together. And when I speak in my anointing, it will be the Father speaking through me, in me as a part of me. I am connected to the Father in a very special way.

It is through my own individual anointing from the Holy Spirit's spiritual gifts that I see what I see and hear what I hear that others cannot. We all are so special that we have our own individual spiritual gifts distributed to us by the Holy Spirit for our own special purpose. Oh, Glory to God, how special I am, how special we are! Thank you, Holy Spirit, thank you.

Which scripture is significant to you and your personal experiences? Take a few minutes and reflect on how the scriptures relate in your life. Did a scripture stand out and resonate from within?

Lesson 3: Distribution

In this section, I share many excerpts from my memoirs. Please note that the dates of my memoirs jump around in time, but this is the order that Jesus wanted me to share this information. As you'll see, Jesus had a lot to say! In these sessions, I learned quite a bit from Jesus about the third lesson for *distribution*. We receive the spiritual gifts through the Holy Spirit who distributes and gives them to us as He so desires. The gifts are to be used to help God's people. I receive my guidance through Jesus Christ in my morning prayers as I attend the weekly Charismatic prayer group meetings and discuss the spiritual gifts.

November 23, 2013
Saturday morning prayers

Someone received his gift of tongues. He will tell you at the next prayer meeting. A few other members will also tell you at the next prayer meeting. You will be able to get several more lessons in before the end of the year. You will finish the lessons at the beginning of next year.

Lesson 3 will discuss the Holy Spirit's distribution of the different spiritual gifts that you have received. Some will have one gift, some will have few gifts, and some will have many gifts. You will tell the story of the messages you deliver to the people who do not know they are to receive a message from you. You will tell of your very first message. You will tell of your healing a colleague's leg.

You will only give a few messages due to the timeframe. You will tell them to not compare your gifts to one another. Each person is chosen to do different things just like you have different body parts. Each part of your body has a vital role to play for the body to function properly. You are to be pleased with the gifts you have and received. You are to be obedient to the Word. Do as you are told. You will be rewarded for your good deeds.

The members will want to hear what you have to say. They are fascinated with your gifts. They are fascinated that they are receiving gifts in the prayer meeting.

You will be a living example of what the Charismatic renewal is all about. You will write books to help with your teachings. You will be asked to be a speaker at different seminars and conferences. You will give testimonies and miracles. You will heal, deliver messages, deliverance, and perform miracles of all kinds. People will marvel at your holiness.

November 26, 2013
Tuesday morning prayers

Your prayer partner is going to give you the scriptures for Lesson 3. Everything is coming along great. Keep up the great work.

December 4, 2013
Wednesday morning prayers

You will go to the prayer meeting. You will have a great time helping to save souls.

December 5, 2013
Thursday morning prayers

You will be pleased tomorrow with the prayer meeting. You will have a great time. You will give them Lesson 3. They will love it.

Some people from another church will come and ask for healing and you will heal them. After tomorrow night, no one will doubt your holiness. The word will spread. You will be pleased with it all. You will have a great time tomorrow helping to save souls and making people happy.

Do not be afraid of the prayer leader. I will run the prayer meeting on Friday. I will tell you what to do and you will do it. So be it. He will not interrupt you. He will be afraid to. He has already been told of your holiness from the SCRC [Southern California Renewal Communities]. *They know you have spiritual gifts, and the priest knows he will be working with you. He knew when he saw you at the Friday prayer meeting. He felt warmness come from your head when he was praying over you. He knew then it was confirmation of your holiness.*

Friday is a big night for you. There will be visitors from other parishes, and they will be very happy to see your holiness. They will go back to their parishes and spread the word about a very beautiful holy lady. They will tell of the miracles and the casting out of evil. Word will spread like wildfire. You will be pleased with it all. It will get people ready to want to read your book. You will sell many of your books for years. There is always someone beginning their spiritual gifts and who needs guidance.

December 6, 2013
Friday morning prayers

Your prayer partner will call you this morning with more scriptures for tonight. You will be well equipped to perform the miracles you will perform tonight. You will give several people messages during the prayer meeting and afterwards. You will be pleased how active you will be. The co-prayer leader will love it. She knows it will bring more people to the prayer meeting after they hear about tonight. Tonight, is a very special night. Keep up the great work.

You will focus on tonight when you return. You will be very pleased with it all. You are going places. You will have a great time. You will be ahead of your game wherever you go. People are going to want to know who you are. So, you tell them. You are a prophet, a mighty, mighty prophet. You will help save the world from the evil that is trying to get an edge on God. It will lose every time. God is the almighty powerful spirit alive in existence.

You will be rewarded for it all. You will always receive favor from Me, Jesus Christ.

Keep going. Everything will work out. You are moving in the right direction.

December 6, 2013
Friday evening prayer group meeting

I went to the prayer meeting. During sharing time, I talked about the different spiritual gifts and how Jesus distributed them according to His will. They will not be evenly distributed. Some people will have one spiritual gift, while others may have more than one. It is done according to your obedience. God will test you.

During our prayer time, the co-prayer leader begins by speaking in tongues and giving a message right afterwards. After she finishes, I usually give a message from Jesus. I start by saying, "There is someone in this room." The messages vary. Sometimes I may say, "There is someone in this room who has been praying very hard." Then I deliver the message to the specific person, but they are never aware that they will receive an answer. It is interesting because when I deliver the message, I won't necessarily remember the message I give in the prayer meeting or the message word for word.

Jesus has told me to not worry about how the person receives the message. My responsibility is to just deliver the message. I do not explain the message or help the person to interpret the message. Jesus told me that a person will know whether it is their message or not. A person will know what they asked for. If a person doubts or questions, then that person needs to pray to Jesus for confirmation.

My Testimony

I share two testimonies, both that happened prior to Lesson 3, as the date indicates.

July 10, 2013
Wednesday morning prayers

Your colleague is not feeling well. He will talk to you today. He will ask you to pray for him and his health. When you pray for him, you will heal him. He will feel a tingling all over his body. When you finish praying, he will not feel any pain and he will feel great. He knows what you did for him. He is going to tell his colleagues who are on the same spiritual level. They will come to you to let you know that they know how holy you are. I will tell you what to say and do.

That day, I went to work as usual and got there early enough to go to the staff room for coffee. I spoke to my colleague in passing in the hallway. I asked him how he was feeling, and he said, "I'm not feeling too well. Can you keep me in your prayers?"

I raised my eyebrows and said, "Oh?" *Was this what Jesus was communicating with me,* I thought. My colleague said he was not feeling well in general, but his leg was bothering him the most. "As you get older, your body parts just don't work the same. You know?" he joked. We both laughed.

We went into the staff room, and as I was making a pot of coffee, I asked my colleague if he would mind if I prayed over him.

He was very receptive of me praying over him. I laid hands on him by touching his head as he bowed in front of me. I spoke in tongues. When I finished, he immediately said, "Oh my God, I have no pain! I felt a tingle in my leg and the pain is gone!"

"Alleluia," I said, and he said, "Amen."

He thanked me for helping him. I told him it was not I who helped him, but the Father above. It was God who did all the work. My colleague then thanked me for being obedient to God. As I finished making the pot of coffee, my mind was racing with so many thoughts.

I found it interesting because my colleague is not a Christian, but he does believe in God. I noticed that Jesus told me to say "God" and not "Jesus Christ." God is so good! Thank you, Jesus, for using me as your vessel for all those who believe in you, our God.

July 11, 2013
Thursday morning prayers

Your colleague is feeling better this morning. He will not be limping. He will have no pain. He knows why he is feeling so good. He is going to thank you for all you did for him yesterday. He will tell you that he did have pain in his left leg. You will remind him that it was God who did all of the work.

Jesus gave me the spiritual gift of healing. I was so pleased that I could be the vessel that God used to heal my colleague. Thank you, Jesus, for the spiritual gift of healing.

The Seven Keys for *Distribution*

Lesson 3, "Distribution," discusses how God distributes His spiritual gifts as He so desires. The seven keys help us to understand the responsibility that goes along with distribution.
The seven keys for *Distribution* are *distribution, comparison, performance, quantity, obedience, being tested,* and *irrevocable.*

1. **Distribution**: Your spiritual gifts are distributed and/or chosen according to God's will.
2. **Comparison**: Do not compare your spiritual gifts to one another.
3. **Performance**: Each person is chosen to perform their spiritual gifts.
4. **Quantity:** The number of spiritual gifts will not be evenly distributed.
5. **Obedience**: Distribution is done according to your obedience.
6. **Being Tested**: God will test you.
7. **Irrevocable**: Your gifts are irrevocable.

Key 1: Distribution

God determines which spiritual gift(s) you will receive. Be happy with what He gives you. All of the charismatic spiritual gifts are important: *wisdom, knowledge, faith, healing, mighty deeds, prophecy, discerning of spirits, tongues,* and *the interpretation of tongues.* God knows what you are willing to give up and sacrifice for Him. If anyone wishes to in order to follow Jesus, you must give up all of you (Mark 8:34).

The Holy Spirit gave me the gifts of prophecy, discerning of spirits, and tongues.

> God added his testimony by signs, wonders, various acts of power, and distribution of the gifts of the Holy Spirit according to his will. (Heb. 2:4)

Key 2: Comparison

It is not a contest of who will get the most spiritual gifts or who will be the most holy. The spiritual gifts are individual according to what God wants you to do. He sees the whole scheme of things. He knows how to fit you into the master plan. Accept your gifts and use them wisely.

> I, then, a prisoner for the Lord, urge you to live in a manner worthy of the call you have received, with all humility and gentleness, with patience, hearing with one another through love, striving to preserve the unity of the spirit through the bond of peace: one body and one spirit, as you were also called to the one hope of your call; one Lord, one Faith, one Baptism; one God and Father of all and in all. (Eph. 4:1–6)

Key 3: Performance

You have been chosen by God to perform different things with your spiritual gifts. Each spiritual gift is related to the church and its function. God's people are one body, and you are chosen to fit into one of the body functions of Christ. Whatever gift you are given, perform it well. To prepare to use your gift(s), you must fast and pray. Remember that the gift is for God's people and not yours. You are given your gift according to God's will.

> To each individual the manifestation of the Spirit is given for some benefit. To one is given through the Spirit the expression of wisdom; to another the expression of knowledge according to the same Spirit; to another faith by the same Spirit; to another gift of healing by the one Spirit; to another discernment of spirits; another variety of tongues. But one and the same spirit produces all of these, distributing them individually to each person as he wishes. (1 Cor. 12:7–11)

Key 4: Quantity

Quantity is the number of spiritual gifts you will receive. Spiritual gifts will not be evenly distributed. You may not receive every spiritual gift; you may only get one or two of them. No matter how many you get, make sure you serve God's people well with them. Accept what God has given you and serve Him well. You should be proud of serving Him with whatever spiritual gifts you receive.

> But one and the same spirit produces all of these, distributing them individually to each person as he wishes. (1 Cor. 12:11)

Key 5: Obedience

Oftentimes people pray for spiritual gifts, but they may not be obedient enough to receive them. You will have assignments to do even when you do not feel like it. To serve God, you must hear Him. Listen to His Word and be obedient. It takes discipline to do God's work. Your spiritual gifts are not a part-time job; it is 24/7. You are on call anytime of the day or night, and you must be obedient to do God's will.

One evening I went shopping for a red blouse for an event the following week. I was driving to the mall when Jesus came to me and said, "You will go now to visit a woman to get rid of evil in her home." I knew who she was, and I had her phone number. Jesus wanted me to call her, and He would tell me what to say. For a moment, I thought about rushing to the mall to buy the blouse before I spoke to the woman, but I had to listen to Jesus. He said *now*. So, I called the woman. I had chosen to be obedient and follow His instructions. I purchased the blouse a few days later. Obedience is important and timing is everything. I am on God's time, not mine.

> I urge you therefore, brothers, by the mercies of God, to offer your bodies as a living sacrifice, holy and pleasing to God, our spiritual worship. Do not conform yourselves to this age but, be transformed by the renewal of your mind, that you may discern what is the will of God, what is good and pleasing and perfect. (Romans 12:1–2)

Key 6: Being Tested

God will test you. He will test you and see how faithful you are to Him. He will see if you can withstand the test of your spiritual gift. Who said it would be easy? This is a commitment to God.

Early one morning during my prayers, Jesus had given me an assignment to deliver a message to a church member later that morning. So, after prayer, I had to get up and get dressed right away to be on time. Low and behold, the prayer member did not attend church.

It was interesting. I could have stayed home because she did not come anyway. No harm no foul, right? But if Jesus asked me to deliver a message again, would I stay home and enjoy my day off because the person may not come?

When I had another assignment to go to church to deliver a message again on one of my days off from work, I asked myself, "Should I go?" What would you do? Well, I went to church, and through the grace of God, I was able to deliver the message this time.

God tests us to see if we are going to be faithful and obedient to His Word regardless of the outcome of the message or the assignment you are to perform.

> Consider it all joy, my brothers, when you encounter various trials, for you know that the testing of your faith produces perseverance. And let perseverance be perfect, so that you may be perfect and complete, lacking in nothing. (James 1:2–4)

Key 7: Irrevocable

Your spiritual gift is irrevocable. Once you receive your spiritual gift, there is no turning back. Make sure you use your gifts wisely and for good in serving God's people.

So, what does it mean when I say that your spiritual gift is "irrevocable"? Well, let's say I was a vessel for Jesus and healed a person. But then I have not been a vessel for Jesus in a long time, maybe even for months. If Jesus wants to use me again several months from now or even several years from now, I still have the anointing and I am a vessel Jesus can use. I will always have the spiritual gift of healing for life.

> For the gifts and the call of God are irrevocable. (Romans 11:29)

Summary

Lesson 3, "Distribution" is the third spoke of the Spiritual Wheel of GOD (the Gifts of Development). The seven keys are *distribution, comparison, performance, quantity, obedience, being tested,* and *irrevocable.*

The spiritual gifts are distributed according to God's will. Do not compare your gifts to one another. Each person is chosen to perform different spiritual gifts.

Spiritual gifts will not be evenly distributed. It's not about the quantity of gifts, but how you use them to serve God. Distribution is done according to your obedience. God will test you to see how faithful you are to Him. Once you receive your spiritual gift(s) there is no turning back because the gifts are irrevocable.

Chapter 4
Lesson 4: Faith

"But without faith it is impossible to please him, for anyone who approaches God must believe that he exists and that he rewards those who seek him." ~*Hebrews 11:6*

You must have faith to receive your spiritual gift(s). You must believe you can not only receive it, but also have the faith that you can do it. It is done unto you as you believe. With faith it can be done (Matthew 8:13).

Faith is the fourth spoke in the Spiritual Wheel of GOD (the Gifts of Development). God lets us know we must be a believer to have faith to receive a spiritual gift.

We hear about faith a lot in our spiritual journey, but how deeply have you looked at and explored the concept of faith? I did not experience the test of my faith in God until the Lord asked me to cast out demons in three women at a prayer meeting, and I had to do it all by myself. I was in my prayer meeting wondering what the prayer members would think of me. I worried they would think I was crazy. At that moment, I prayed for Jesus to give me the strength and the faith to believe in Him enough to do it. Through the grace of God, I was able to do it. It was at that moment I truly understood what it meant to have faith in God.

In this chapter, I provide the scriptures Jesus gave to my prayer partner and in the order, she had given to me. I share the testimony of my faith with my prayer group about the time when Jesus commanded me to deliver a message to the church service greeter and heal her to walk without her cane. Finally, I discuss the seven keys of Lesson 4 that will help you understand your responsibility in serving God's people through your faith.

Scriptures for Faith

The scriptures in this lesson speak to faith and how you will receive rewards according to your deeds. Those who acknowledge Jesus will be acknowledged by God. You are to have faith in Jesus, for He will tell you what to say. To have faith you must believe that God will take care of you and He will lead you in the way you should be led.

> "Amen, I say to you, among those born of women
> there has been none greater than John the Baptist; yet the

least in the kingdom of heaven is greater than he." (Matt. 11:11)

"Whoever receives a prophet because he is a prophet will receive a prophet's reward, and whoever receives a righteous man because he is righteous will receive a righteous man's reward." (Matt. 10:41)

"Therefore, do not be afraid of them. Nothing is concealed, nor secret that will not be known. What I say to you in the darkness, speak in the light; what you hear whispered, proclaim on the housetops . . . Everyone who acknowledges me before others I will acknowledge before my heavenly Father. But whoever denies me before others, I will deny before my heavenly Father." (Matt. 10: 26–27, 32–33)

"When they hand you over, do not worry about how you are to speak or what you are to say. You will be given at that moment what you are to say. For it will not be who speak but the Spirit of your Father speaking through you." (Matt. 10:19–20)

"This is the one about whom it is written: 'Behold, I am sending my messenger ahead of you; he will prepare your way before you.'" (Matt. 11:10)

And their people brought to him a paralytic lying on a stretcher. When Jesus saw their faith, he said to the paralytic, "Courage, child, your sins are forgiven." (Matt. 9:2)

When he entered the house, the blind men approached him, and Jesus said to them, "Do you believe that I can do this?" "Yes, Lord," they said to him. Then he touched their eyes and said, "Let it be done according to your faith." (Matt. 9:28–29)

Jesus turned around and saw her and said, "Courage, daughter! Your faith has saved you." and from that hour the woman was cured. (Matt. 9:22)

And Jesus said to the centurion, "You may go; as you have believed, let it be done for you." And at that very hour [his] servant was healed. (Matt. 8:13)

Then he said to his disciples, "The harvest is abundant, but the laborers are few; so, ask the master of the harvest to send out laborers for his harvest." (Matt. 9:37–38)

"Beware of false prophets, who come to you in clothing, but underneath are ravenous wolves." (Matt. 7:15)

"Do to others whatever you would like to have them do to you. This is the law and the prophets." (Matt. 7:12)

"Ask and it will be given to you; seek and you will find; knock and the door will be opened for you." (Matt. 7:7)

"Just so, every good tree bears good fruit, and a rotten tree bears bad fruit. A good tree cannot bear bad fruit, nor can rotten tree bear good fruit . . . So, by their fruit you will know them . . . Everyone who listens to these words of mine and acts on them will be like a wise man who built his house on rock." (Matt. 7:17–18, 20, 24)

"Stop judging that you may not be judged. For as you judge, so will you be judged, and the measure with which you measure with which you measure will be measured out to you. (Matt. 7:1–2)

"Therefore, I tell you, do not worry about your life, what you will eat [or drink], or about your body, what you will wear. Is life more than food and the body more than clothing? . . . All these things the pagans seek. Your heavenly Father knows that you need them all . . . Do not worry about tomorrow; tomorrow will take care of itself. Sufficient for a day is its own evil." (Matt. 6:25, 32, 34)

"But I say to you, love your enemies, and pray for those who persecute you . . . For if you love those who love you, what recompense will you have? Do not the tax collectors do the same? And if you greet your brothers only, what is unusual about that? Do not pagans do the same? So be perfect, just as your heavenly Father is perfect." (Matt. 5:44, 46–48)

"But when you pray, go to your inner room, close the door, and pray to your Father in secret. And your Father who sees in secret will repay you." (Matt. 6:6)

"Rejoice and be glad, for your reward will be great in heaven. Thus, they persecuted the prophets who were before you . . . Just so, your light must shine before others, that they may see your good deeds and glorify your heavenly Father." (Matt. 5:12, 16)

> He said to them, "Come after me, and I will make you fishers of men." (Matt. 4:19)
>
> Thus, says the Lord, your redeemer, the Holy One of Israel: "I am the Lord, your God, teaching you how to prevail, leading you on the way you should go." (Is. 48:17)

Discussion of Scriptures for Faith

This chapter has some of my favorite scriptures that I refer back to over and over again! Isn't it beautiful when God tells us that He loves us and has our back? That we shouldn't worry when He is by our side? Having faith means having so much love for Jesus and knowing that He will always be with you.

The scriptures that resonated for me were Matthew 7:7 and 10:19–20, and Isaiah 48:17. I know I need to ask the Lord for what I want and then let go and let God's will be done. I must always seek Jesus to follow Him and to serve His people well. For seeking the Lord, I shall find Him and all my needs. I also know I must do my part, and as I go out into the world, I know the opportunities will appear and I will find what I need to do God's work.

In the beginning, when God would give me an assignment, He told me my assignment in detail. I worried if I would know what to do, or if I would remember what to say because He would talk to me for hours at a time. In the beginning, Jesus would tell me not to worry about what to say. He told me I would be given what to say at that given moment because it would not be my words but the words of God speaking through me. That was awesome! Jesus helped me not to worry about what to say. I just had to have the faith in Him to deliver the messages, and He did.

When I read Isaiah 48:17, I take a deep breath to take it all in. Jesus Christ is our Lord. He is leading me in the way so I can help God's people. Who would know better than God to lead His people and to lead me but God Himself? I must have faith to allow God to lead me.

Which scriptures in this chapter are significant to you and your personal experiences? Take a few minutes and reflect on how the scriptures relate in your life. Did a scripture stand out and resonate from within?

Lesson 4: Faith

I'm so excited to share my experiences with you for this lesson on faith! I had such beautiful conversations with Jesus about faith and how

He was to use me to share His message. Jesus was very clear on what He wanted me to do.

December 7, 2013
Saturday morning prayers

In Lesson 4, you will speak on faith. You must have faith to receive your spiritual gifts. You must believe that you have them. It is truly done unto you as you believe. You were given many gifts of faith. You will give them an example of one of your spiritual gifts of faith. You will give the testimony on your faith to believe enough to deliver the first message, and to do as I commanded of you to do with the church service greeter. You had to have faith to do as you were told to do. You will say to them, "Some of you really want to speak tongues, but you really don't believe you can speak them and therefore you can't."

In 1 Corinthians, the prophecy is for the believer because you must have faith in God to believe. Your prayer partner will give you scriptures to prepare you for Lesson 4.

December 13, 2013
Friday morning prayers

You have arrived. You are now ready to do some things in the prayer meeting. You will give them Lesson 4. You will be very pleased. Do not be afraid of the prayer leader. There is nothing he can do about it. You are doing My will. I am your God. I am telling you how to help save souls. You will be listened to. You will be pleased with tonight. You have several messages to give to individuals. They will be pleased with their messages, including the co-prayer leader.

Your Lesson 4 is about having to believe that people can receive spiritual gifts. If they do not believe they can have it, they will not. They all know it is done unto you as you believe. It is one thing to know it and another to believe what you know. You will give your testimonies tonight along with the lesson they are to learn. You will be very pleased with the miracles that are going to take place.

You have the gift of knowledge, so you know many things. You will be very pleased with it all. Sometimes you will know things, but you will not say anything about it unless I want it said. You are not to say everything that you know.

You also have the gift of wisdom to know what to do with your knowledge. You are a very powerful prophet. People can see your holiness. They want to be your friend. They want to talk to you. They want to know what you know. They want to get advice from you. You will be very pleased with it all. Keep up the great work.

In Lesson 4, you will give the testimony of the church member. You will tell of your first assignment after hands were laid on you. You will tell of how you first started your ministry without really knowing your ministry. Your prayer partner will give you scriptures. She will have a lot of them. You will read them all before going to the prayer meeting.

You will get five lessons in this year [2013]. *You will do the remaining five lessons the first part of next year* [2014]. *While you are working on your second religious book, you will be publishing your first one. It will be such a big hit that they are going to want to read your second book and go to your workshops. You will do a workshop at the SCRC conference in 2014.*

[I published my first book, *Look What Happened to Me. Is It Happening to You Too?* in October 2014 after the SCRC Conference, which was in August 2014. I did not do a workshop at the SCRC conference in 2014.]

December 13, 2013
Friday evening prayer group meeting

I discussed Lesson 4 on faith with my prayer group that evening. We sat around in a circle and shared our stories. When it was my turn, I felt my heart flutter with excitement. I was eager to share my story.

You must believe you can receive your spiritual gift. You must want it and pray for it. You will receive your gift(s) according to God's will. Jesus had given several members the gift of tongues. The gift is irrevocable. They have the gift, but at the time they did not believe they had it. He told them they must have faith so they could receive their gifts.

Jesus told me not to worry that the members wouldn't be able to speak tongues. Some would be able to speak tongues by the week that followed. I was so excited that the members would be able to speak tongues. I know Jesus will distribute other gifts too.

My Testimony

Please note that my testimony in 2013 overlaps with another prayer meeting that occurred on October 16, 2009, with the Life in the Spirit Seminar group at my parish church where the priest laid hands on us to receive our spiritual gifts from God. My testimony is from that day in 2009. I first want to share what Jesus told me in October 2009, and then I share my 2009 testimony with my prayer group in 2013.

October 18, 2009
Sunday morning prayers

Now you are beginning to use your gifts more precisely with others. You will begin to pray every day for those who need God's help that they will receive it. You will be told whom you will help. They may or may not know that they even need the help, but you will know. Today a person will approach you from church who will need God's help. She will confide in you her troubles. You will lay hands on her and say a prayer to uplift her spirit. At the time, I will tell you the words to say. Do not be afraid that she will not welcome it because she will. She will immediately feel relief. It will be the beginning of healing her soul. Go now in peace.

Wow! I had never laid hands on anyone nor ever thought I had the anointing to do so. I knew I had to have the faith that I could do this. I knew it is done unto you as you believe, and that I must have the faith in God that I could. I prayed for God to give me the faith I needed to carry out His assignment. I knew I had to have the courage to do it and I did. I got ready for Mass services and went to church on Sunday, October 18, 2009. It was the eleven a.m. Mass.

As I entered the church, I said good morning to the greeter at the front door. She had been the greeter to members at the parish for several years. After Mass, there was an announcement that the seventh-grade class was selling doughnuts and coffee. I thought that was a good opportunity for someone to come up to me because it would be light and casual.

I purchased two twist donuts and a cup of coffee. I sat down at an empty table so I could wait for someone to come up to me. After a few minutes, the greeter came over and sat down. "So, you were the one to get the twist doughnuts," she said with a smile. I offered her one of them, but she shook her head. "I got a cherry-filled one, which is good enough for me," she said.

We made small talk for a little bit. The greeter talked about her arthritis. Then a woman sat down at the end of the table. The table was set cafeteria style where there were long rectangular tables. The woman sat on the end, and me and the greeter sat in the middle across from each other.

Toward the end of our conversation, the woman talked about needing knee surgery.

Wow, I thought. *Is this the woman Jesus wants me to heal?*

"You could also get surgery for your arthritis," the woman said to the greeter.

The greeter chuckled. "Oh no, no, no. I'm afraid of anesthesia," she said. "I'm worried that when they put me to sleep, I might not ever wake up!"

The greeter went on to say, "I will be eighty in January." The woman said, "my father had surgery in his eighties, and he was now in his nineties. Well, it was nice chatting with you," she said, and she got up and left.

The greeter and I continued talking for a little bit. She told me she was going to the bus stop so she can go shopping at the mall. Then it hit me. I knew then that the greeter was the one Jesus wanted me to help, not the other woman. That I would lay hands on her before she got out of my car when I dropped her off at the mall.

I offered to take her to the mall, and she said, "You don't have to take me to the mall."

"The Lord blessed me with a car, and He is blessing you by giving you a ride to the mall."

The greeter smiled. She then felt more comfortable accepting the ride to the mall rather than taking the bus.

"I'll go get the car, so you don't have to walk far," I said. She used a cane to walk, so she was grateful.

As we drove to the mall, we saw the bus drive by. "That's my bus," the greeter said. "I would have missed the bus and would have had to wait for another bus for over thirty minutes because the bus runs slower on Sundays."

I told her that I was taking the Life in the Spirit Seminar on Fridays at our church. I started the conversation, but it shifted to something else. She told me her name was in Italian, but she used the English version. I told her my name was Jacquie, and my spiritual name is Dr. Jacquie. It was funny how long we knew each other from church but never knew each other's name.

As I pulled into the parking lot of the mall, she told me to pull in the handicap space because she had a handicap sticker and wouldn't take that long. So, I did.

Something came over me, and it felt like the right morning to bring up what Jesus had told me. "I am taking the Life in the Spirit Seminar on Fridays here at church," I mentioned again. "Well, last Friday the priest laid hands on the members of the seminar after Mass that evening. The priest preached about serving God, not being served. I was praying this morning, and Jesus told me a person was going to come to me and tell me her problems. He told me I was going to lay hands on this person and that the person would welcome it."

The greeter broke into a huge smile. "Yes!" she exclaimed.

We held hands. I let go of one of her hands and placed my right hand on her head. Then I prayed over her using her Italian name.

I don't remember what I said, but I do remember that Jesus said not to worry about what to say for I would know what to say when I was ready to say it. The greeter was wearing sunglasses, and when I finished, she removed her sunglasses to show me her tears of joy. She thanked me and proceeded to get out of the car.

Wow! I kept thanking Jesus for allowing me to lay hands on someone. This stuff was happening pretty fast. I could hardly believe that the priest had laid hands on me on Friday, and by Sunday I was laying hands on someone else. Thank you, Jesus, for choosing me to be a vessel to help the souls here on Earth. In Jesus' name, Amen.

Laying hands on someone for the first time was one of the hardest things for me to do in my spiritual quest. My faith was tested, and I thank God for giving me the faith I needed to complete His assignment. I had to have faith to do as I was told to do.

What I learned from this experience, is that, to have faith you must believe. I had to believe God exist and that he can do all things. I then had to have the faith in God that I was the vessel for God to do His work. In 1 Corinthians, prophecy is for the believer because you must have faith in God to believe.

The Seven Keys for Faith

The Lord presents us with seven keys in Lesson 4 to help us understand our responsibility in serving God's people through faith. You must believe that you can receive the spiritual gifts.

The seven keys in Lesson 4 are *belief system, spiritual gifts, self-identity, faith, believe, measure,* and *know.*

1. **Belief System**: Believe you can do it and you can receive it.
2. **Spiritual Gifts**: Believe in your spiritual gifts and not worry about what others have.
3. **Self-Identity**: You are who you believe you are.
4. **Faith**: To believe is to have faith.
5. **Believe**: To have faith is to believe.
6. **Measure**: To measure a person's worth is to measure a person's deeds.
7. **Know**: To know it is done unto you as you believe and have faith that it will be done.

Key 1: Belief System

Everything is done unto you as you believe. If you do not believe, you cannot achieve. Faith is so simple but so hard to ascertain. Your belief system is what makes up your world because your belief system is what you believe is true. Therefore, you must believe that God is real, that He exists.

A Christian belief system is when you believe in the supernatural beings such as the Trinity, God the Father, the Son our Lord and Savior, and the Holy Spirit. We believe in after life, heaven, Purgatory, and hell. We communicate to God through prayer. We have a moral code of ethics and church rituals that we practice our religion along with sacred objects and symbols.

For example, I attend weekly church services to pray together, receive the Holy Communion that represents the body of Jesus Christ, and to practice the Holy Sacraments. You create your world through your faith by responding and fulfilling from your truth, your belief system. You must believe in God to be able to receive the charismatic spiritual gifts from the Holy Spirit.

> But without faith it is impossible to please him, for anyone who approaches God must believe that he exists and that he rewards those who seek him. (Hebrews 11:6)

Key 2: Spiritual Gifts

Do not compare yourself to others. You are here to develop your soul. You came by yourself and you will leave and be accountable by yourself. God knows what's best for you. Keep going. You must believe that you can perform the spiritual gift you have received. You must also know you are only the vessel, the instrument that God uses to perform the spiritual gift. God works within you.

The spiritual gifts are the charismatic gifts of the Holy Spirit to build up the body of Christ. The charisms (spiritual gifts) are supernatural gifts. They are graces of the Holy Spirit where they can directly or indirectly benefit the church. These spiritual gifts are distributed to you according to the Holy Spirit as He so desires. To receive charisms, you will need to be baptized in the spirit having a special relationship with the Holy Spirit. In 1 Corinthians 13, Paul tells us that you may have the spiritual gifts (charisms) but if you do not have love, you cannot sanctify anyone. Without love, it will not profit you.

In 1 Corinthians 12: 4, Paul says there are differences of spiritual gifts but from the same spirit, and differences of ministries but the same Lord. The spiritual gifts are given to you for the profit of God's church. To reiterate, the charismatic spiritual gifts are wisdom, knowledge, faith, healing, miracles, prophecy, discernment of spirits, various type of tongues, and interpretation of tongues.

Wisdom is the understanding of the Word of God. One time I chaperoned at a teen conference and the teens would try to sneak out to hang out after curfew. They were to be in their own rooms in the dorm by ten p.m. A few of them wanted to hang out after curfew, but one of them did not want to go. She tried to tell them it was not a good idea, but they went anyway. The teen who did not go had the wisdom to stay behind. Sure enough, the teens who broke the rules got caught. When you just know what to do, this is wisdom.

The word of knowledge is when you have knowledge from the Holy Spirit, and you may have a message for someone. An example of knowledge is when you know you have a message for someone whether you knew the person or not. You will go up and deliver the message to them. You may or may not see that person again.

Faith is being able to believe in God. It is having a close relationship and confidence in Him. For example, in your prayers, you just believe that the Lord hears you and your prayers will be answered. I know a young woman who can pray for a person and she will get the answer in her prayers for them. The night before she goes to sleep, she prays for the person and she then she receives the answer for that person the very next morning. When she prayed to the Lord, some answers would come to her quickly while others took longer or may be still pending. She has the gift of faith. She believes in God with all her heart knowing it is done under you as you believe.

Healing can be done differently according to how the Holy Spirit wants to use you. You can lay hands on a person by touching or holding your hand above them or stretched out to them and pray over them. You can pray for them even if they are not present with you. Some churches have "prayer warriors" who pray with the person needing prayer. Prayer warriors often have the gift of tongues.

A miracle is a supernatural event that cannot be proven naturally or scientifically such as exorcisms, healings, levitations, stigmata, etc.

Prophecy can predict future events or general statements that build up the church. Paul says in 1 Corinthians 14:1, 3, and 4: "Pursue love, and desire spiritual gifts, but especially that you may prophesy . . . . he who prophesies speaks edification and exhortation and comfort to men . . . he who prophesies edifies the church."

I recall one time in prayer meeting when I gave a message and said, "Someone in the room is going to receive unexpected money and will give it all away." The members sort of chuckled when they heard the message. Two weeks later, a member won the church school raffle ticket for $2,000 and gave the money back to the school scholarship fund.

Discernment of spirits allows a person to be able to discern between spirits, a person, and things about them. For example, a person may walk into a home and can discern if evil spirits are there. Someone with this spiritual gift would be able to look at a person and know if they have evil influence on them, or if they are holy in the grace of God.

When you have the gift of tongues, you do not speak to people but directly to God. With this gift, the person edifies him or herself unless he or she interprets them to the church. Your tongues may not sound like any other. The tongues may be of another language, dialect or just sounds.

I remember when I received the gift of tongues. I was in the Life in the Spirit Program at my church. There was a guest speaker that evening at the prayer meeting. The priest had the members stand up to form a circle and sing alleluia over and over. Two of us received the gift of tongues that night. I had my eyes closed as I sang "alleluia." The next thing I knew the priest was touching my shoulder and whispered, "Lower your voice." I opened my eyes and realized I was shouting and speaking in tongues. I was amazed because I wasn't expecting to receive them, and I did not realize I was saying them.

The interpretation of tongues interprets (explain) the tongues that were spoken for the church to understand; therefore, the tongues edify the church. In my experience, I am able to interpret two phrases of my singing tongues.

My interpretation is "I love the Lord, the Lord. I love the Lord, the Lord. I love the Lord for this day. I love the Lord, the Lord. I love the Lord, the Lord. I love the Lord and give praise."

Now, I say my "singing tongues" because I have different type of tongues. One type of tongue is singing, but I have exorcism, praying, speaking, healing, prophecy, and intercession tongues as well. Each one has its own sounds and dialect.

> Since we have gifts that differ according to the grace given to us, let us exercise them: if prophecy, in proportion to the faith; if ministry, in ministering; if one is a teacher, in teaching; if one exhorts, in exhortation; if one

> contributes, in generosity; if one is over others, with diligence; if one does acts of mercy, with cheerfulness. (Rom. 12:6–8)

Key 3: Self-Identity

Your self-identity is formed from your belief system. Your self-identity can be on non-spiritual levels and/or spiritual levels. In a non-spiritual way, your self-identity and your belief system are powerful. You are who you believe you are. If you feel dumb and stupid, no matter how many times someone says you are intelligent, you will not believe them because your belief system says you're not. So, when a person calls you "dumb," it will reinforce your belief system. It will hurt, and you will feel pain or maybe even anger. You must monitor your feelings and your belief system.

An example of the spiritual self-identity, I could say: "I believe in the Trinity: The Spirit of God the Father, the Son (our Lord and Savior), and the Holy Spirit. I believe God has a spirit that I am connected to and is a part of me. I am allowing God to use me as His vessel to write this book to educate His people regarding the spiritual gifts of the Holy Spirit. I am also one of His prophets and spiritual teachers."

> For God so loved the world that he gave his only son, so that everyone who believes in him might not perish but might have eternal life. (John 3:16)

Key 4: Faith

To believe you must have faith in yourself and God. You must believe in something and act upon your faith. You cannot have faith without believing in it. You must search your belief system for the truth. You need to know what you believe in. Who are you? Who do you want to be? Do you believe in yourself that you can achieve it? Do you believe in Jesus Christ? Do you believe in God? Do you have a purpose? Do you have a ministry?

The key to getting closer to God and to hearing the Holy Spirit speak to you from within is through your faith that you know you can do it. You can believe you can hear the Holy Spirit, but it is your faith that will allow you to be able to learn how to hear the Holy Spirit. Not only must you believe it can be done, but you have to believe through your faith that you can do it. To believe in yourself is to have faith in yourself.

> Jesus said to them in reply, "Have faith in God. Amen, I say to you, whoever says to this mountain, 'Be lifted up and thrown into the sea,' and does not doubt in his heart but Believes that what he says will happen, it shall be done for him.
>
> Therefore, I tell you, all that you ask for in prayer, believe that you will receive it and it shall be yours." (Mark 11:22–24)

Key 5: Believe

Are you getting it now? You must have faith and belief to use your spiritual gift(s). You can believe in something, but it doesn't mean you will achieve it. You must be true to yourself. Have you ever believed that you couldn't do something because you do not have faith in yourself that you can do it? Maybe it's learning a musical instrument, or being promoted at work, or even losing weight. You know that you *want* to do those things to better yourself, but if you don't *believe* that you can achieve it you will never reach your goal. You will never achieve anything without having faith in yourself that you can do it.

> Whatever you ask for in prayer with faith, you will receive. (Matt. 21:22)

Key 6: Measure

To measure a person's worth is to measure a person's deeds. Your deeds (actions) come from your belief system. You cannot do anything without believing you can do it. Your worth is who you are. Your deeds tell who you are. If a person is always kind and giving, what would that tell you about that person? Just identify the deeds of a person and you will know them.

> But we will not boast beyond measure but will keep to the limits God has apportioned us, namely, to reach even to you. (2 Cor. 10:13)
>
> Peter [said] to them, "Repent and be baptized, every one of you, in the name of Jesus Christ for the forgiveness of your sins; and you will receive the gift of the Holy Spirit." (Acts 2:38)

Key 7: Know

Know that it is done unto you as you believe and have faith that it will be done. Listen to your inner voice of God. You must have faith in God and know that He will guide you, protect you, take care of you, and provide all of your needs. To trust in God, you must have faith in Him.

> Jesus said to them in reply, "Have faith in God." (Mark 11:22)
>
> If you remain in me and my words remain in you, ask for whatever you want, and it will be done for you. (John 15:7)

Summary

Lesson 4, "Faith," is the fourth spoke of the Spiritual Wheel of GOD (the Gifts of Development). We must have faith in order to use our spiritual gifts in the way that God wants us to.
The seven keys are *belief system, spiritual gifts, self-identity, faith, believe, measure,* and *know.*

Everything is done unto you as you believe. To believe is to have faith you can do it and you can receive it. Do not compare yourself to others. Believe in your spiritual gifts and don't worry about what others have. Your belief system is powerful. You are who you believe you are. To believe is to have faith, and to have faith is belief. You must have faith in yourself and God. To measure a person's worth is to measure a person's deeds. Your deeds come from your belief system. It is done unto you as you believe, have faith that it will be done, and you will achieve it.

Chapter 5
Lesson 5: Dedication

"No one can serve two masters. He will either hate one and love the other or be devoted to one and despise the other. You cannot serve God and mammon." ~Matthew 6:24

When you think about the word "dedication," what is the first thing that comes to mind? I always think about being dedicated to my relationship with Jesus and my family, all of which takes work! You can't expect to have a flourishing and healthy relationship without putting in some effort. It takes time and dedication.

Dedication is the fifth spoke in the Spiritual Wheel of GOD (the Gifts of Development). God wants you to be committed and loyal in dedicating yourself to your spiritual gifts.

In Lesson 5, I share the scriptures in the order that my prayer partner gave to me. I also share my testimony about the time I tried to deliver a message to someone who never showed up to Mass service. Then I discuss the seven keys of dedication, which will help you to understand your responsibility in serving God's people through dedication and devotion to your spiritual gift(s).

Scriptures for Dedication

In these scriptures, Jesus communicates the need for His believers to have dedication to Him and God's Word. The scriptures in this lesson describe dedication in various ways. For example, we are to be merciful and do not judge nor condemn. You are to give, and gifts will be given to you. Bless those who curse you and pray for those who mistreat you. Also, do good to those who do good to you. The scriptures speak to the parable of a sower who went out to sow his seeds.

The scriptures also speak to the blessed who are the ones who hear God's words and observe them, acknowledge God before others, and rejoice for the right reasons. The scripture also says the Father in Heaven will give the Holy Spirit to those who ask Him.

> ". . . for nothing will be impossible for God." (Luke 1:37)
>
> Then the angel said to her, "Do not be afraid, Mary, for you have found favor with God." (Luke 1:30)

Mary said, "Behold, I am the handmaid of the Lord. May it be done to me according to your word." Then the angel departed from her. (Luke 1:38)

"Blessed are you who believed that what was spoken to you by the Lord would be fulfilled." (Luke 1:45)

". . . to shine on those who sit in darkness and death's shadow, to guide our feet into the path of peace." (Luke 1:79)

John answered them all, saying, "I am baptizing you with water, but one mightier than I is coming. I am not worthy to loosen the thongs of his sandals. He will baptize you with the Holy Spirit and fire . . . and the Holy Spirit descended upon him in bodily form like a dove. And a voice came from heaven, "You are my beloved Son; with you I am well pleased." (Luke 3:16, 22)

Then astonishment seized them all and they glorified God, and struck with awe, they said, "We have seen incredible things today." (Luke 5:26)

"Be merciful, just as [also] your Father is merciful. Stop judging and you will not be judged. Stop condemning and you will not be condemned. Forgive and you will be forgiven. Give and gifts will be given to you; a good measure, packed together, shaken down, and overflowing, will be poured into your lap. For the measure with which you measure will in return be measured out to you." (Luke 6:36–38)

"But to you who hear I say, love your enemies, do good to those who hate you, bless those who curse you, pray for those who mistreat you . . . Do to others as you would have them do to you. For if you love those who love you, what credit is that to you? Even sinners love those who love them. And if you do good to those who do good to you, what credit is that to you? Even sinners do the same." (Luke 6:27–28, 31–33)

When Jesus heard this, he was amazed at him and, turning, said to the crowd following him, "I tell you, not even in Israel have I found such faith." (Luke 7:9)

"And blessed is the one who takes no offense at me." (Luke 7:23)

"I tell you, among those born of women, no one is greater than John; yet the least in the kingdom of God is greater than he." (Luke 7:28)

But he said to the woman, "Your faith has saved you; go in peace." (Luke 7:50)

"A sower went out to sow his seed. And as he sowed, some seed fell on the path and was trampled, and the birds of the sky ate it up. Some seed fell on rocky ground, and when it grew, it withered for lack of moisture. [7]one seed fell among the thorns, and the thorns grew with it and choked it. And some seed fell on good soil, and when it grew, it produced fruit a hundredfold." After saying this, he called out, "Whoever has ears to hear ought to hear." (Luke 8:5–8)

Then his disciples asked him what the meaning of this parable might be. He answered, "Knowledge of the mysteries of the kingdom of God has been granted to you; but the rest, they are made known through parables so that they may look but not see and hear but not understand." (Luke 8:9–10)

"This is the meaning of the parable. The seed is the word of God. Those on the path are the ones who have heard, but the devil comes and takes away the word from their hearts that they may not believe and be saved. Those on rocky ground are the ones who, when they hear, receive the word with joy, but they have no root; they believe only for a time and fall away in time of trial." (Luke 8: 11–12)

"As for the seed that fell among thorns, they are the ones who have heard, but as they go along, they are choked by the anxieties and riches and pleasures of life, and they fail to produce mature fruit. But as for the seed that fell on rich soil, they are the ones who, when they have heard the word, embrace it with a generous and good heart, and bear fruit through perseverance . . . For there is nothing hidden that will not become visible, and nothing secret that will not be known and come to light. Take care then, how you hear. To anyone who has, more will be given, and from the one who has not, even what he seems to have will be taken away." (Luke 8:14–15, 17–18)

He said to her, Daughter, your faith has saved you; go in peace." . . . On hearing this, Jesus answered him, "Do not be afraid; just have faith and she will be saved." (Luke 8:48, 50)

Then they set out and went from village to village proclaiming the good news and curing diseases everywhere . . . About eight days after he said this, he took Peter, John, and James and went up the mountain to pray. (Luke 9:6, 28)

While he was praying, his face changed in appearance and his clothing became dazzling white . . . who appeared in glory and spoke of his exodus that he was going to accomplish in Jerusalem. Peter and his companions had been overcome by sleep, but becoming fully awake, they saw his glory and the two men standing with him. Luke 9:29, 31–32)

As they were about to part from him, Peter said to Jesus, "Master, it is good that we are here; let us make three tents, one for you, one for Moses, and one for Elijah." But he did not know what he was saying. (Luke 9:33)

While he was still speaking, a cloud came and cast a shadow over them, and they became frightened when they entered the cloud. Then from the cloud came a voice that said, "This is my chosen Son; listen to him." (Luke 9:34–35)

"Nevertheless, do not rejoice because the spirits are subject to you, but rejoice because your names are written in heaven." (Luke 10:20)

"And I tell you, ask and you will receive, seek and you will find; knock and the door will open for you . . . If you then, who are wicked, know how to give good gifts to your children, how much more will the Father in heaven give the Holy Spirit to those who ask him?" (Luke 11:9, 13)

Turning to the disciples in private he said, "Blessed are the eyes that see what you see. For I say to you, many prophets and kings desired to see what you see, but did not see it, and hear what you hear, but did not hear." (Luke 10:23–24)

He replied, "Rather, blessed are those who hear the word of God and observe it. (Luke 11:28)

"There is nothing concealed that will not be revealed, nor secret that will not be known. Therefore, whatever you have said in the darkness will be heard in the light, and what you whispered behind closed doors will be proclaimed on the housetops . . . Even the hairs of your head have all been counted. Do not be afraid. You are worth more than many sparrows." (Luke 12:2–3, 7)

"I tell you, everyone who acknowledges me before others the Son of Man will acknowledge before the angels of God. But whoever denies me before others will be denied before the angels of God." (Luke 12:8–9)

"Everyone who speaks a word against the Son of Man will be forgiven, but the one who blasphemes against the Holy Spirit will not be forgiven . . . and the servant that was ignorant of his master's will but acted in a way deserving of a severe beating shall be beaten only lightly. Much will be required of the person entrusted with much, and still more will be demanded of the person entrusted with more." (Luke 12:10, 48)

"Blessed is that servant whom his master on arrive finds him doing so. (Luke 12:43)

Discussion of Scriptures for Dedication

I love how many times Jesus tells us, "Do not be afraid." It's only natural for us to feel fear, some people more than others. But in the scriptures above, Jesus reminds us that He is always there for us, even when we are frightened. We cannot let fear or anxiety, or weakness get in the way of using our spiritual gifts. This is the "dedication" we have committed as believers in Christ.

The scripture that stood out to me is Luke 1:45. It brought back the memory of a recovering alcoholic student who had evil around her. Jesus told me that I would be the vessel to remove the evil from her and it happened. What He told me was fulfilled.

One morning, Jesus spoke to me for three hours, but it did not seem that long. Even now, Jesus will speak to me in my morning prayers anywhere from one to three hours depending on the assignments and information He wants to provide for me. On that particular morning, Jesus spoke to me about someone in one of my classes who was struggling with her class assignments and staying focused in class lectures. He mentioned some of the problems she was struggling with had to do with drinking and that she went to Alcohol Anonymous meetings. She had been struggling with evil spirits around her. Her counselor was not helping her with the evil spirits because she was afraid to talk about them. When she tried to speak about it with her counselor, she could not open her mouth—the words would not come. Jesus told me I would get rid of the evil spirit around her. He said I would speak tongues until it was gone. He also said I would know when they were gone, and I was to tell the student, "The evil is gone, and it will never return. You can now sleep at night."

The interesting thing when Jesus speaks to me and gives me assignments is that He doesn't always give a specific name or person. He told me, "You will know when it is the one by what they say." I teach several day and night classes. Jesus did not tell which class. I was excited to find out. I knew it could happen any time and in either class.

Several weeks went by. I had to be patient. I knew God had spoken and to let His will be done. I knew what Jesus told me would be fulfilled, and it was. Several weeks later, Jesus answered the student's prayer and removed the evil in him after class that night. As I spoke tongues, the student said she felt a tingling all over her body until the tongues stopped. She felt the evil leave her body.

Which scriptures are significant to you and your personal experiences? Take a few minutes and reflect on how the scriptures relate in your life. Did a scripture stand out and resonate from within?

Lesson 5: Dedication

In this section, I share excerpts from my memoirs with Jesus during my morning prayers. My communication with Jesus at this time was plentiful! To be honest, I didn't realize at the time how much dedication would play a factor in my spiritual journey until Jesus pointed it out to me.

Jesus told me how my life was changing. I used to wonder if I was worthy of His holiness to use me as His vessel. I am just an ordinary person, born into a family of eight children as the second born. Jesus would lead me and direct me through each lesson.

In the excerpts, Jesus provided instructions on Lesson 5, "Dedication," for preparation of the prayer meeting. After I arrived home from the meeting, Jesus also spoke to me in prayer. I wanted to get feedback so desperately from Jesus about how well I performed the assignment given to me. Jesus is so good! Along with the instructions and feedback, He always provides encouragement to keep me going. Oh, Jesus, I want to surrender to you. I want to dedicate my life to you in helping to save souls.

December 16, 2013
Monday morning prayers

Your life is changing. You will be very happy with it all. You have the prayer group where you want them now. They are listening, and the spiritual gifts are beginning to come to some of the members. They listened and took what you said seriously. All of them are praying for the spiritual gifts and they will receive them. They do not know how holy the prayer group is right now. They will receive special gifts during the ten lessons. Several of the members will write their testimony about receiving their gifts during the ten lessons distribution. You will be very pleased, and you will be very happy to write the book. It will be very successful. They are going to love to have their testimony in the book.

You are doing great. Everything is going to work out. Your prayer partner will give you the scriptures for Lesson 5. You will be pleased.

December 20, 2013
Friday morning prayers

You will have an exciting night tonight. You will give Lesson 5 on dedication and devotion to do God's work. You will explain how you must be committed to do the work of your gift. You must be devoted to God and know that God is your source. You must be obedient to His Word as you use your gift for His people. You will give your testimony of that time when you went to church on a rainy morning to give someone a message, but the person did not come to church. You must be dedicated and devoted to God enough to do things even when it feels uncomfortable. You will give the testimony of the time you had to chase people down to give your messages even when they did not know you were going to give them a message. Your dedication and devotion to God will help you to stay focused on your gifts and using them in the right way and for the right reasons. Your gifts are for God's people, not for you.

December 20, 2013
Friday evening prayer group meeting

That night I went to the prayer meeting. During sharing time, I relayed Jesus' message about dedication. You must be dedicated and devoted to performing your spiritual gift for God. You must be committed to practicing your gift according to what God wants you to do and at the time He wants it done. I then shared my testimony about the time when I went to eight-o'clock Mass on a rainy morning to share Jesus' message, but the person didn't show up.

Once again, we all sat in a circle and went around the room. When it was my turn, I said in a confident voice, "devote my life to Jesus no matter the time or place." Then I shared my testimony.

My Testimony

One morning in November 2009, my alarm clock went off and I made myself get out of bed. It was gray clouds and cold, and I didn't really want to venture out in the weather. I was teaching at the time, and I had a few days off during the week where I didn't have to lecture, and it was nice to sleep in.

As I was getting dressed, I yawned and felt a bit sluggish, but then I learned quickly that I had spiritual work to do on my days off. Jesus needed me to do His work! I did not get the luxury of sleeping in and just relaxing on my day off. Very often, Jesus gave me assignments for the eight-a.m. Mass during the week, regardless of whether it was on a rainy day. He wanted me to give messages to people even though they didn't know they were going to receive a message. Jesus used me to heal people who didn't even know they were going to be healed. You must have dedication and devotion for God to follow Jesus. You must be committed to doing God's work. That day, I put on my raincoat and braved the weather because that was what I had to do. I needed to share Jesus' message, but the woman didn't even come to Mass.

After everyone shares their testimony, we have prayer time. Everyone stands up in a circle in front of their chairs, and the co-prayer leader begins with prayer and prophecy. Jesus usually gave me messages during prayer time.

In that prayer meeting, Jesus told me to repeat to the group His messages:

Jesus said to me, "There is someone in this room who has been praying for tongues for a very long time. Yes, it is time, but use the gift wisely."

Jesus continued, "There is someone in this room whose child will heal. You must follow the doctor's orders precisely."

Another prophecy, as Jesus said, "There is someone in this room who is very, very sad. You just pretend to be happy on the outside. Your prayers will be answered."

Jesus said, "There is someone in this room who is afraid. Do not to be afraid. I am with you. I will protect you."

After prophecy comes prayer requests, and it was a beautiful night of prayer and celebration. Jesus sure did have a lot to say on that night!

After arriving home from the prayer meeting, I wanted to talk to Jesus about what had happened at the meeting. I asked Him what He thought about the prayer meeting.

You did a good job tonight. A child, who can now speak tongues, is afraid to speak tonight. They will at the next prayer meeting.
[This did not happen].

They will call the prayer leader before the prayer meeting, and they will tell her that they can speak tongues. She will speak tongues over the phone to the prayer leader. The prayer leader will then call to let you know what has occurred.
[This did not happen.]

Both prayer leaders will be very happy. They will call the Charismatic Renewal Director to let him know what is happening. He will also be very pleased with what is going on. More and more members will attend the prayer meeting. You will become more and more popular. People are going to come to see you. A prayer group member wanted to talk to you but was not comfortable talking to you in front of the prayer leader. She is not aware that the prayer leader has changed his opinion about you. She will see you at church. She will talk to you then.

Lesson 5 went well. Even though it appeared like they were not listening, they were. They heard every word you said. They are looking forward to their gifts. In 2014, the gifts will start pouring in. They will be amazed at your special gifts. I say "gifts" because they will see you perform many. Both prayer leaders know where you are going with this, and they are pleased to be a part of it. It has rejuvenated the prayer group. They were surprised to have so many prayer members on the last Friday of the year. They will be more surprised at how many will start off the new year. The word is out that you are helping to give spiritual gifts to the prayer members. More people will start coming.

Everything is going to work out. Keep going. We will talk later. Go now. Go in peace for I, Jesus Christ, have spoken. Amen!

The Seven Keys for Dedication

Lesson 5, "Dedication," provides us with many ways to help us stay focused on what God is asking of us. The seven keys help us understand our responsibility in serving God's people through dedication and devotion to Him.

The seven keys are *devotion, willingness, performance, challenge, special, commitment,* and *wise.*

1. **Devotion**: Be dedicated and devoted to your spiritual gift.

2. **Willingness**: You must be willing and ready to perform your spiritual gift no matter what.
3. **Performance**: Perform your spiritual gift when Jesus tells you to do so.
4. **Challenge**: You will be challenged not to perform your gift, but you must do it anyway.
5. **Special**: Spiritual gifts are special and should be treated as such.
6. **Commitment:** Spiritual gifts should be taken seriously.
7. **Wise**: Dedicate your life to using your gift(s) wisely.

Key 1: Devotion

"Dedication" is to commit yourself to something. You must commit yourself to Jesus. You have a responsibility, and you want to be devoted to God and to your spiritual gift. To be devoted, you must be loyal to God through Jesus Christ. You must give up your life to walk with Jesus through dedication and devotion.

> Then Jesus said to his disciples, "Whoever wishes to come after me must deny himself, take up his cross, and follow me. For whoever wishes to save his life will lose it, but whoever loses his life for my sake will find it." (Matt. 16:24–26)

Key 2: Willingness

When you commit yourself with loyalty to God our Lord Jesus Christ, you must fulfill your assignments through your spiritual gift(s) even when you do not feel like it. You have to be willing and ready to answer the call. If you are preparing for a marathon, you practice for hours, dedicating yourself to the workout even when you do not feel like it. That is willingness to show up to the task and do what you need to do in order to be successful.

> What profit would there be for one to gain the whole world and forfeit his life? Or what can one give in exchange for his life? For the Son of Man will come with his angels in his Father's glory, and then he will repay everyone according to his conduct. (Matt. 16:26–27)

Key 3: Performance

You will perform the gift at the precise time that the Holy Spirit tells you to. You do not decide what would be a more convenient time to do it. Timing is important. It may not mean anything to you, but God has a purpose for you, and it is to be done at the time He wants it done, not when you feel like it. Remember, it is not you who are performing the gift but Jesus Christ who does all the work. You are the vessel that He uses.

> For we are his handiwork, created in Christ Jesus for the good works that God has prepared in advance, that we should live in them. (Eph. 2:10)

Key 4: Challenge

Some assignments that God gives you may be a challenge. There will be days when you will be challenged to not perform your gift, but you must do it anyway. For instance, the spiritual gift of prophecy. Maybe you don't know if what you say will happen and you feel afraid to say it. It may be a challenge for you to just open your mouth to say the words. Or the spiritual gift of healing. You may think it is not the right place or time to lay hands on someone, so it may be a challenge for you. As they say, "feel the fear and do it anyway."

> I have the strength for everything through him who empowers me. (Phil. 4:13)

Key 5: Special

Your spiritual gift(s) is special and tailor-made for your personality and experiences. You should treat it as special because it is.

For example, you have the anointing to receive messages from God. How do you receive them? Some may hear the Holy Spirit through thoughts, some from dreams (sight), some from hearing (audio), and some telepathically (just know). Even in those categories, there are still uniqueness based on your personality and experiences.

> "Indeed, I wish everyone to be as I am, but each has a particular gift from God, one of one kind and one of another." (1 Cor. 7:7)

> To each individual the manifestation of the Spirit is given for some benefit. To one is given through the Spirit the expression of wisdom; to another the expression of knowledge according to the same Spirit; to another faith by the same Spirit; to another gifts of healing by the one Spirit; to another mighty deeds; to another prophecy; to another discernment of spirits; to another a variety of tongues; to another interpretation of tongues. But one and the same spirit produces all of these, distributing them individually to each person as he wishes. (1 Cor. 12:7–11)

Key 6: Serious

You must take your spiritual gift seriously. It is not to be played with and treated like a toy. For example, you have the gift of healing. Like a toy, you are excited when you first receive your spiritual gift. You want to heal every chance you get. After you have had the gift for a while, you are no longer thrilled with your gift of healing. So, like a used toy, you set aside your spiritual gift of healing by not going to church-healing services or attending Charismatic prayer meetings. You must do your assignment when you are told to do so even if your spiritual gift is not new and fun anymore.

> . . . but sanctify Christ as Lord in your hearts. Always be ready to give an explanation to anyone who asks you for a reason for your hope. (1 Peter 3:15)

Key 7: Wise

There is a story about the wise, old owl who knows a lot and pays attention down to the smallest detail. The success is in the details. When you are given an assignment, pay attention to the details and be loyal, devoted, and dedicated.

You must use your gifts wisely and sensibly and do them as you are told by the Holy Spirit. You must commit yourself to using your gift with obedience.

> As each one has received a gift, use it to serve one another as good stewards of God's varied grace. Whoever preaches, let it be with the words of God; whoever serves, let it be with the strength that God supplies, so that in all things God may be glorified

> through Jesus Christ, to whom belong glory and dominion forever and ever. Amen. (1 Peter 4:10–11)

Summary

Lesson 5, "Dedication," is the fifth spoke of the Spiritual Wheel of GOD (the Gifts of Development). The seven keys needed are *devotion, willingness, performance, challenge, special, commitment,* and *wise.*

You must be dedicated and devoted to your spiritual gift. That is, you must be loyal and committed to your spiritual gifts for God through the Holy Spirit. You are not to perform your gift only when you feel like it. Timing is important. You will perform your gift when the Holy Spirit tells you to do so.

Remember, it is not you who is performing the gift, but the Holy Spirit that does all the work. You are the vessel that He uses. There will be days when you will be challenged to not use your gift, but you must do it anyway. Your gift is special and should be treated as such. You do your assignment when you are told to do so even if your spiritual gift is not new and fun anymore. You must dedicate and devote your life to using your gift wisely and how the Holy Spirit instructs you to use it.

This is the conclusion of Part I, "Understanding Spiritual Gifts." The lessons in Part I are *preparation* (Lesson 1), *people* (Lesson 2), *distribution* (Lesson 3), *faith* (Lesson 4), and *dedication* (Lesson 5).

Part II, "Implementing Spiritual Gifts," will include lessons on *work, listening, obedience, ministry,* and *spirituality.*

Part II: Implementing Spiritual Gifts

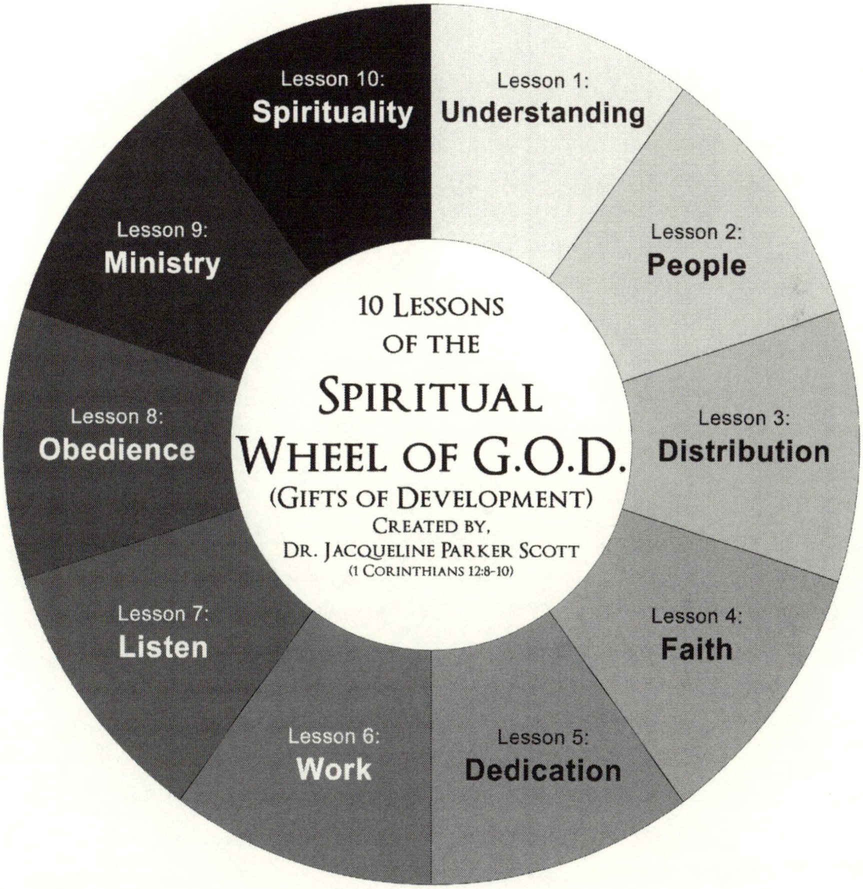

Chapter 6
Lesson 6: Work

"For we are his handiwork, created in Christ Jesus for the good works that God has prepared in advance, that we should live in them." ~ Ephesians 2:10

You have a spiritual gift, but you now must work to help save souls. Who said it would be easy? You will need to fulfill your spiritual gift responsibility of work just like you would if you had an earthly nine-to-five job commitment.

Work is the sixth spoke in the Spiritual Wheel of GOD. God wants you to take your spiritual gift(s) seriously and responsibly, and now it is time to put your feet to the fire, so to speak. You need to act, to put in the work, to make all of this possible.

In Lesson 6, I share the scriptures that my prayer partner gave me in the order that the Holy Spirit had given to her. I share my testimony of how I, as a vessel of God, healed a man's hand, and the man did not know God was going to heal it. Finally, I discuss the seven keys, which will help you understand your responsibility in serving God's people through work commitment to your spiritual gift(s).

Scriptures for Work

The scriptures in this lesson show examples of the work it took to spread the Word of God. For example, when the Apostles were in Jerusalem, they heard that Samaria had accepted the Word of God. Peter and John were given the assignment (work) to go there and pray for them. Work was given Philip when he reached Azotus and went about claiming the good news to all the towns until he reached Caesarea. Saul preached in Damascus, Peter restored Tabitha to life, and there was also the baptism of Cornelius. It was also in the scriptures that the disciples were first called "Christians" in Antioch.

> Bless the Lord my soul; all my being, bless his holy name! Bless the Lord, my soul; and do not forget all his gifts, Who pardons all your sins, and heals all your ills, Who redeems your life from the pit, and crowns you with mercy and compassion, Who fills your days with good things, so your youth is renewed like the eagle's. (Ps. 103:1–5)

Give the thanks to the Lord for he is good, his mercy endures forever! . . . Sent forth his word to heal them and snatched them from the grave. (Ps. 107:1, 20)

Better to take refuge in the Lord than to put one's trust in mortals. (Ps. 118:8)

I disclosed my ways and you answered me; teach me your statutes. Make me understand the way of your precepts; I will ponder your wondrous deeds . . . Give me understanding to keep your law, to observe it with all my heart. Lead me in the commandments, for that is my delight. (Ps. 119:26–27, 34–35)

I thank you for you answered me; you have been my savior . . . This is the day the Lord has made; let us rejoice in it and be glad . . . Give thanks to the Lord, for he is good, his mercy endures forever. (Ps. 118:21, 24, 29)

Now when the apostles in Jerusalem heard that Samaria had accepted the word of God, they sent them Peter and John, who went down and prayed for them, that they might receive the Holy Spirit, for it had not yet fallen upon any of them; they had only been baptize in the name of the Lord God. Then they laid hands on them and they received the Holy Spirit . . . (Acts 8:14–17)

Then Philip opened his mouth and, beginning with the scripture passage, he proclaimed Jesus to him . . . *And Philip said, "If you believe with all your heart, you may," And he said in reply, "I believe Jesus Christ is the son of God." Then he ordered the chariot to stop, and Philip and the eunuch both went down into the water, and he baptized him. (Acts 8:35, 37*–38)

[*Acts 8:37. The oldest and the best manuscripts of Acts omits this verse, which is a Western text reading.]

When they came out of the water, the Spirit of the Lord snatched Philip away, and the eunuch saw him no more, but continued on his way rejoicing. Philip came to Azotus and went about proclaiming the good news to all the towns until he reached Caesarea. (Acts 8:40)

But Peter and the apostles said in reply, "We must obey God rather than men . . . We are witnesses of these things, as is the Holy Spirit that God has given to those who obey him." (Acts 5:29, 32)

Now Saul, still breathing murderous threats against the disciples of the Lord, went to the high priest and asked him for letters to the synagogues in Damascus, that, if he should find any men or women who belonged to the Way, he might bring them back to Jerusalem in chains. (Acts 9:1–2)

On his journey, as he was nearing Damascus, a light from the sky suddenly flashed around him. He fell to the ground and heard a voice saying to him, "Saul, Saul, why are you persecuting me? He said, "Who are you sir?" The reply came, "I am Jesus, whom you are persecuting. Now get up and go into the city and you will be told what you must do." The men who were traveling with him stood speechless, for they heard the voice but could not see no one. Saul got up from the ground, but when he opened his eyes, he could see nothing; so, they led him by the hand and brought him to Damascus. For three days he was unable to see, and he neither ate nor drank. (Acts 9:4–9)

There was a disciple in Damascus named Ananias, and the Lord said to him in a vision "Ananias." He answered, "Here I am, Lord." The Lord said to him. "Get up and go to the street called Straight and ask at the house of Judas for a man from Tarsus named Saul. He is there praying, and [in a vision] he has seen a man named Ananias come in and lay [his] hands on him, that he may regain his sight." (Acts 9:10–12)

But Ananias replied, "Lord, I have heard from many sources about this man, what evil things he has done to your holy ones in Jerusalem. And here he has authority from the chief priests to imprison all who call upon your name." But the Lord said to him, "Go, for this man is a chosen instrument of mine to carry my name before Gentiles, kings, and Israelites, and I will show him what he will have to suffer for my name." (Acts 9:13–16)

So, Ananias went and entered the house; laying his hands on him, he said, "Saul, my brother, the Lord has sent me, God who appeared to you on the way by which you came, that you may regain your sight and be filled with the Holy Spirit. (Acts 9:17)

Immediately things like scales fell from his eyes and he regained his sight. He got up and was baptized, and when he had eaten, he recovered his strength. (Acts 9:18–19)

He stayed some days with the disciples in Damascus, and he began at once to proclaim God in the synagogues, that he is the son of God. (Acts 9:20)

Now in Joppa there was a disciple named Tabitha (which translated means Dorcas). She was completely occupied with good deeds and almsgiving. Now during those days, she fell sick and died, so after washing her, they laid [her] pit in a room upstairs . . . Peter sent them all out and knelt down and prayed. Then he turned to her body and said, "Tabitha, rise up." She opened her eyes, saw Peter, and sat up. He gave her his hand and raises her up, and when he had called the holy ones and the widows, he presented her alive. This became known all over Joppa, and many came to believe in the Lord. (Acts 9:36–37, 40–42)

. . . what has happened all over Judea, beginning in Galilee after the baptism that John preached, how God anointed God of Nazareth with the Holy Spirit and power. He went about doing good and healing all those oppressed by the devil, for God was with him. (Acts 10:37–38)

This man God raised (on) the third day and granted that he be visible . . . He commissioned us to preach to the people and testify that he is the one appointed by God as judge of the living and the dead. To him all the prophets bear witness, that everyone who believes in him will receive forgiveness of sins through his name. (Acts 10:40, 42–43)

While Peter was still speaking these things, the Holy Spirit fell upon all who were listening to the word. (Acts 10:44)

. . . and when he had found him, he brought him to Antioch. For a whole year they met with the church and taught a large number of people, and it was in Antioch that the disciples were first called Christians. (Acts 11:26)

While they were worshiping the lord and fasting, the Holy Spirit said. "Set apart for me Barnabas and Saul for the work to which I have called them. Then completing their fasting and prayer, they laid hands on them and sent them off. (Acts 13:2–3)

So, they sent forth by the Holy Spirit, went down to Seleucia and from there sailed to Cyprus. When they arrived in Salamis; they proclaimed the word of God in the Jewish synagogues. They had John also as their assistant. When they had traveled through the whole island as far as Paphos, they met a magician named Bar-Jesus who was a Jewish false prophet . . . But Saul, also known as Paul, filled with the Holy Spirit, looked intently at him . . . (Acts 13:4–6, 9)

They appointed presbyters for them in each church and, with prayer and fasting, commended them to the Lord in whom they had put their faith. (Acts 14:23)

"Do not be afraid. Go on speaking, and do not be silent, for I am with you. No one will attack and harm you, for I have many people in this city." (Acts 18:9–10)

He said to them, "Did you receive the Holy Spirit when you became believers?" They answered him, "We have never even heard that there is a Holy Spirit." He said, "How were you baptized? They replied, "With the baptism of John." . . . Altogether there were about twelve men . . . So extraordinary were the mighty deeds God accomplished at the hands of Paul that when face cloths or aprons that touched his skin were applied to the sick, their diseases left them, and the evil spirits came out of them. (Acts 19:2–3, 7, 11–12)

Then some itinerant Jewish exorcists tried to invoke the name of the Lord God over those with evil spirits, saying, "I adjure you by the God whom Paul preaches." When the seven sons of Sceva, a Jewish high priest, tried to do this, the evil spirit said to them in reply, "God I recognize, Paul I know, but who are you?" (Acts 19:13–15)

I persecuted this Way of death, binding both men and women and delivering them to prison . . . On that journey as I drew near to Damascus, about noon a great light from the sky suddenly shone around me. I fell to the ground and heard a voice saying to me, "Saul, Saul, why are you persecuting me?" I replied, "Who are you sir?" And he said to me, "I am God the Nazorean whom you are persecuting." (Acts 22:4, 6–8)

My companions saw the light but did not hear the voice of the one who spoke to me. I asked, "What shall I do sir?" The Lord answer, "Get up and go into Damascus, and there you will be told about everything appointed for you to do." (Acts 22:9–10)

Since I could see nothing because of brightness of that light, I was led by hand by my companions and entered Damascus. A certain Ananias, a devout observer of the law, and highly spoken of by all the Jews who lived there, came to me, and stood there and said, "Saul, my brother, regain your sight." And at that very moment, I regained my sight and saw him. Then he said, "The God of our ancestors designated you to know his will, to see the Righteous One, and to hear the sound of his voice; for you will be his witness before all to that you have seen and heard. Now, why delay? Get up and have yourself baptized and your sins washed away, calling upon his name." (Acts 22:11–16)

Then he brought them out and said, "Sirs, what must I do to be saved?" And they said, "Believe in the Lord God and you and your household will be saved." So, they spoke the word of the Lord to him and to everyone in his house. He took them in at that hour of the night and bathed their wounds; then he and all his family were baptized at once. (Acts 16:30, 31–33)

There is no partiality with God. (Rom. 2:11)

Discussion of Scriptures for Work

We all have work to do! What I love about these scriptures is how they speak about the glory of God and how He pardons our sins and heals us. He gave us mercy and compassion. The scriptures show how the apostles would work for the Lord by going to the towns and spreading the good news. One of the scriptures resonated in me was in Acts: 9:17.

The Lord sent Ananias to lay hands on Saul so he could regain his sight. It was not Ananias who healed Saul's eyes so that he could see again; it was God who healed Saul. Ananias was the vessel that God worked through to heal him.

We are vessels that Jesus works through to do His work helping His people. For I know it is not I, writing this book, but it is Jesus Christ working through me. I am His vessel, and He uses us to deliver messages and to help His people. I cannot take credit for God's work. I can only take credit for the work I do as His vessel.

Which scriptures are significant to you and your personal experiences? Take a few minutes and reflect on how the scriptures relate in your life. Did a scripture stand out and resonate from within?

Lesson 6: Work

In this section, I share excerpts of my memoirs with Jesus. He had a lot to say about how we need to put in the work and effort to fulfill our promises to Him. He gave me encouragement and direction on presenting it.

January 9, 2014
Thursday morning prayers

You will present Lesson 6 tomorrow. You will be very pleased with it all. You will do a good job. You already have Lesson 6 scriptures. Members are listening to you. You will be pleased with your work on Friday. You will have several messages for the members. The prayer leaders will be pleased too.

January 10, 2014
Friday morning prayers

You will give them Lesson 6. You will read Lesson 6 prayers and scriptures before you go to the prayer meeting tonight. You will be pleased with tonight. People will listen to you. They want to have their spiritual gifts.

[I received the scriptures from my prayer partner, and I read them just before I went to the prayer meeting. I went over all the materials and information for Lesson 6.]

January 10, 2014
Friday evening prayer group meeting

I delivered the message to the prayer group for Lesson 6. They listened to me and they heard what I said. They needed to know that it was work to help save God's people. It's not all glamorous in what you do to help save souls. It may not always be a convenient time for you to serve God. But because you are serving out your purpose, you will enjoy the work you do. It is work to take your gifts seriously. God will only use you as much as you allow Him to. I proceeded to discuss my testimony, the healing of a prayer member's hand.

January 11, 2014
Saturday morning prayers

The prayer members understood Lesson 6 on work. They are understanding what you are saying. As their gifts begin to come, they will give glory to God, and they will thank God for you being in their lives and for being obedient to God. Everything is working out. You will be very pleased with it all.

My Testimony

This testimony happened several years prior to writing this book, but it is appropriate to mention because it demonstrates how given assignments are work even when you are attending your regular routine of earthly activities. You are always on call, so to speak, in doing God's work in helping to save souls.

As mentioned, this testimony happened several years prior to the prayer meeting. On January 2, 2010, I was told I would have to get up and go to the church for the eight o'clock Mass services in order to complete the healing assignment given to me. On my days off from work, I usually sleep in and catch up on my rest, but not on that day! I was working for God.

January 2, 2010
Saturday morning prayers

The Living Faith message this morning is "keep the faith." "Let what you hear . . . remain in you" (1 John 2:24). I am so lucky to have the faith to have God within me. Thank you, God, for choosing me.

"Good morning, dear Jesus. Do you have anything to say?"

Yes. There's work to do this morning. Today you will go to church for the eight o'clock Mass. A prayer member is sick. He has been sick for some time now. He is going to approach you after Mass today. He is going to ask if you can help him. You will say yes. Don't worry about what you are going to say. I will let you know. You will lay hands on him to heal him. He is going to feel better immediately. He is going to thank you. You must remember to say, "It is not I but the Father above. God did it.

So that morning I went to the eight o'clock Mass as I was instructed. After Mass, I stayed in my seat and prayed the Rosary with the prayer group, but I wasn't sitting with them. After the Rosary, I left the church from the back entrance. I waited outside until the prayer group finished their meeting as I was instructed by God. Our plans on that morning had to be adjusted slightly. When they finished, God told me to start walking slow.

I walked around from the front of the church to the side of the church towards the parking lot slowly as instructed. Just then, a man exited the side door. I knew he was the one. He was the only prayer member talking to some women who were in the Rosary meeting. They walked out to the parking lot. The two women went their way. The prayer member was walking alone. I called out his name and he turned around. I walked up to greet him.

"How are you are doing this morning?" I asked.

He said he wasn't doing too well. He was having trouble with his hand. He had skin cancer and had been going to the doctor for treatment, but it wasn't healing. "I go back to the doctor on Friday," he said.

"Can I pray over you?" I asked.

"Yes, of course you can," he said.

So, I prayed over him in tongues. Afterwards, I told him that I would continue praying for him. He thanked me for my prayers and left.

When I returned home, I was very curious about what God would think about how things went with the prayer member. It didn't go exactly the way God said it would go, so I asked him about it.

"Dear God, may I ask you a question? How did everything go today?"

Yes. You did a good job. The plans changed slightly, but you adjusted well. The cancer on the prayer member's hand is gone. By Friday it will not be there. He is going to thank you because the doctors are going to ask him what he did. He is going to tell them that you laid hands on him to make the cancer go away. You really understand how it goes. You will be rewarded for all your work that you do for Me, your Lord, your God.

I felt so relieved that everything had worked out! I was working for God!

January 3, 2010
Sunday morning prayers

The next morning, I prayed as I usually did, and God once again told me how proud He was of my efforts from the day before.

Miracles can only happen if you believe. I am glad that you know how it works now. You have a free will to accept the miracle that I give you. So, know, Dr. Jacquie, that you did your job. You obeyed. Everything went as planned. You did your part.

It was good for me to hear God say I did my job. I know I am not to be concerned with the outcome. That is up to the person receiving the message.

January 8, 2010
Friday evening prayer group meeting

I attended the prayer meeting following the healing of a prayer member's hand. The prayer member also attended the prayer meeting. When we went around the room to share our testimonies, the prayer member shared that I had prayed over his hand and now his hand was healed. Everyone in the group rejoiced!

"My doctor asked what I did, and I told him that Dr. Jacquie—a prayer member in my prayer group—prayed over me," he said. Then he turned to me and smiled. Tears glistened in his eyes. "Thank you, Dr. Jacquie," he said.

"I'm so glad that you are healed and doing well, but it was not I who healed you but the Father above. It is God who did all the work," I said. The prayer member thanked me for being obedient.

After the prayer meeting, I went home and wanted to ask God how things went. I didn't feel fully confident speaking out in front of the group. Whenever I ask God a question, He always knows before I can even voice the question what I want to ask, and he always answer me.

January 9, 2010
Saturday evening prayers

The next evening after the Friday night prayer meeting, I spoke to Jesus.

"Good evening, dear God, may I ask you a question?"

Yes. You were obedient. You did what I asked of you. The prayer group member now knows that you healed his thumb. You delivered the message correctly. You do not have to worry. The members knew what you were saying, and that it was God's doing who healed him. Go now. Go in peace. God has spoken.

I was pleased that everything went well and that I was obedient to the Word. I clearly understand that I am to do as God tells me and not to worry about how the person receives the message. It is on the person receiving the message to accept or reject it. I also know it takes energy to perform God's work.

The Seven Keys for Work

Lesson 6, "Work," gives us guidance and examples on how we need to work for God. The Lord provided seven keys to help us understand our responsibility in serving God's people through work.

The seven keys are *work, spiritual gifts, fasting, challenge, God's work, faith,* and *knowledge.*

1. **Work**: Know your spiritual gift(s) is work.
2. **Spiritual Gifts**: Perform and take your spiritual gift(s) seriously.
3. **Fasting**: Fast and pray prior to performing your spiritual gift(s).
4. **Challenge**: There will be challenging days to perform your spiritual work.
5. **God's Work**: Do not worry about how you feel to get the job done, for it is God that does all the work.
6. **Faith**: Know that you have been chosen to do the work, therefore, have faith you can get it done and on time.
7. **Knowledge**: Know your work and perform it well.

Key 1: Work

It is more than just knowing your spiritual assignments. You must be able to implement them. You must be able to do the job and do it well to completion. In other words, you must get the job done.

Your spiritual gift is like a job. It is work. You must perform your spiritual gift whether you feel like it or not. You are committed to go to work and be there on time. You are to implement the duties as required of you. You must treat your spiritual gift the same. You must fulfill the obligation of your assignments.

For example, there are different types of job positions. According to the type of position will determine the type of work you will implement. If you are a carpenter, you build homes, furniture, and so on. If you are a healer, you will heal people. You need to know your type of work in order to implement and complete it.

What type of spiritual work you can do? Your spiritual work that we are looking at in this book is the charismatic gifts of the Holy Spirit. Pray to the Holy Spirit to reveal your spiritual gifts to you if you do not already have them.

> For this reason, I remind you to stir into flame the gift of God that you have through the imposition of my

> hands. For God did not give us a spirit of cowardice but rather of power and love and self-control. (2 Tim. 1:6–7)
>
> For we are his handiwork, created in Christ Jesus for the good works that God has prepared in advance, that we should live in them. (Eph. 2:10)

Key 2: Spiritual Gifts

You must take on your spiritual gift as if it were a job and perform your spiritual job seriously. Even if you don't like your job, you should take it seriously. A spiritual job requires even more work and may have unpredictable hours as opposed to a nine-to-five job or set hours.

Let's say you were given the spiritual gift of healing. Your spiritual work will be in the area of healing, not casting out demons, delivering messages, prophesying, teaching, and so on. It's important to understand the type of spiritual gift you have. Your specific spiritual gift will help determine what kind of spiritual work you will have in helping God's people.

The Holy Spirit's charismatic spiritual gifts are in 1 Corinthians 12:8–10. One is given the word through wisdom, the gift of knowledge, faith, the gift of healing, the gift of effecting of miracles, the gift of prophecy, the gift of distinguishing of spirits (discernment), the gift of various kinds of tongues, and/or the gift of interpretation of tongues.

> Be eager to present yourself as acceptable to God, a workman who causes no disgrace, imparting the word of truth without deviation. (2 Tim. 2:15)

Key 3: Fasting

You should always fast and pray before you perform your spiritual gifts.

> "When you fast, do not look gloomy like the hypocrites. They neglect their appearance, so that they may appear to others to be fasting. Amen, I say to you, they have received their reward. But when you fast, anoint your head and wash your face, so that you may not appear to others to be fasting, except to your Father who is hidden. And your Father who sees what is hidden will repay you." (Matt. 6:16–18)

> And we have this confidence in him, that if we ask anything according to his will, he hears us. And if we know that he hears us regarding whatever we ask, we know that what we have asked him for is ours. (1 John 5:14–15)

Key 4: Challenge

There will be days when you will be challenged to implement your spiritual work. You will step up to the challenge and know that the Holy Spirit is with you.

One time, I was attending Sunday Mass and I was kneeling in the church pew. All of a sudden, I started getting a terrible headache. This happened years ago as a young adult. I was going through trusting in Jesus. I knew intellectually what to do. *It is done unto you as you believe,* right? Well, as I sat in church, I was trying to believe God can do anything, including getting rid of my headache.

I sat in the back of the church. I knew this was going to be a challenge for me to test myself and my belief system. I prayed and then I fixated on the church services. I went up to receive Holy Communion. It was a challenge for me to walk up to the alter with my headache. As I received the host—the bread that represented our Lord Jesus Christ—I began to feel a little better. I still had to get back to my seat because the pain was not all the way gone. Through the grace of God, I made it and the pain continued to subside.

Challenges are encounters and obstacles that may get in your way. You will also have challenges as you go about with your anointings serving God's people. You just have to keep going and know the Holy Spirit is with you helping you along the way.

> "For I am the Lord your God who takes hold of your right hand, who says to you, 'Do not fear, I will help you.'" (Is. 41:13)
>
> And it will be said, "Build up, build up, prepare the way, remove every obstacle from the way of my people." (Is. 57:14)

Key 5: God's Work

In doing God's work, you may feel too tired, or maybe you are a little hesitant to do it. You may not feel sure of yourself that you can do it or know what to say.

Do not worry about how you feel to get the job done, for it is God who does all the work. Remember, it is not you who is doing the work, it is God. It is not about you. It is about serving God's people. It is not I, but the Father above. It is Jesus Christ who does all the work. You are the vessel that He uses.

I remember the very first time Jesus used me as His vessel to heal someone. I was not very familiar with the healing process at all. It was one night right after the charismatic prayer group meeting and a member approached me. Sometimes we would fellowship for a little while after prayer meeting. As we were talking, she was moving her arm in a circular motion. She said, "My shoulder is becoming more and more painful. I am not sure what is wrong with it."

Jesus told me to ask her, "Do you mind if I pray over it?"

She said, "Sure, please do." So, I started speaking in tongues until Jesus stopped. I say "Jesus stopped" because I did not know when to stop. Clearly, it was Jesus who healed.

It was like she was in shock. She started grasping for air but then at the same time she said, "My shoulder, the pain is gone away." Little did she know that I was as shocked as she was or maybe even more. Jesus told me to tell her, "It is not I, but the Father above. It is Jesus Christ who does all the work. Jesus healed you."

> I can do all things through Him who strengthens me. (Phil. 4:13)
>
> For nothing will be impossible with God. (Luke 3:37)
>
> Do you not know that your body is a temple of the Holy Spirit within you, whom you have from God, and that you are not your own? For you have been purchased at a price. Therefore, glorify God in your body. (1 Cor. 6:19–20)

Key 6: Faith

Everything begins with having faith that you are anointed and have the spiritual gift that was given to you by the Holy Spirit. Your spiritual gift(s) is the spiritual work you will do for God's people.

You were chosen to perform certain spiritual gifts to serve God's children, therefore, have faith you can get it done. You must receive your assignments, and together with God, you will do them on time. Timing is everything. Your spiritual gifts are scheduled at a certain time, God's time.

In order to do what I do in the spiritual world with my spiritual gifts, I must have faith that I can do it. I believe and have faith that there is a God and that He is real. I have a special relationship with Him. We communicate and collaborate to get the spiritual job done. Without faith, no work can be done. In other words, no faith, no work.

> For we are his handiwork, created in God for the good works that God has prepared in advance, that we should live in them. (Eph. 2:10)
>
> "It was not you who chose me, but I who chose you and appointed you to go and bear fruit that will remain, so that whatever you ask the father in my name he may give you." (John 15:16)

Key 7: Knowledge

Know what your assignment is and perform it well. Take it seriously. Read about your gift and know as much about it as you can.

Now that you have faith that there is a God, you must now know your assignment to get the spiritual job done. You must know how to communicate with the Holy Spirit in order to receive it. You need to know your purpose. Know why you are here. Know what you are doing. Know your ministry. It all comes together. Know your God. Know that He is real. Know who you are; you are part of the spirit of the Lord.

> There are different kinds of spiritual gifts but the same Spirit; there are different forms of service but the same Lord; there are different workings but the same God who produces all of them in everyone. To each individual the manifestation of the Spirit is given for some benefit. (1 Cor. 12:4–7)
>
> As each one has received a special gift, employ it in serving one another as good stewards of the manifold grace of God. Whoever speaks is to do so as one who speaking the utterance of God; whoever serves is to do so as one who is serving by the strength which God supplies; so that in all things God may be glorified through Jesus Christ, to whom belongs the glory and dominion forever and ever. Amen. (1 Peter 4:10–11)

Summary

Lesson 6, "Work," is the sixth spoke in the Spiritual Wheel of GOD (the Gifts of Development). The seven keys needed are *work, spiritual gifts, fasting, challenge, God's work, faith,* and *knowledge.*

It is more than just knowing your spiritual assignments. You must be able to implement them. You must be able to do the job and do it well to completion. In other words, you must get the job done. Get the assignment done.

You must also perform your spiritual gift whether you feel like it or not, and you must perform your spiritual gift seriously. You will fast and pray prior to performing your spiritual gift. Yes, there will be days when you will be challenged to perform your spiritual work, but it's up to you to step up to the challenge and know that the Holy Spirit is with you.

Now that you have faith that there is a God, you must know your assignment to get the spiritual job done. You must know how to communicate with the Lord in order to receive it. You need to know your purpose. Know why you are here. Know what you are doing. Know your ministry. It all comes together. Know your God. Know that He is real. Know who you are; you are part of the spirit of the Lord.

Chapter 7
Lesson 7: Listen

"This rather is what I commanded them: Listen to my voice; then I will be your God and you shall be my people. Walk exactly in the way I command you, so that you may prosper." Jer. 7:23

Listen to what the Holy Spirit has to say. Whether it is the Holy Spirit or God Himself, one must listen to what God has to tell them.

If you have not already, you must develop a relationship so you can hear and communicate with the Holy Spirit. In order to hear your assignments to help serve God's people, you must practice the prayer of listening.

I'm sure you've experienced a time when you were talking to a friend or a loved one about something only to realize that they haven't been listening. Many of us are guilty of doing this! Our minds are racing with thoughts and emotions, and we check out of a conversation sometimes. We're easily distracted. Learning how to listen—*really listen*—takes practice. We can apply this to many areas of our lives, but our relationship with Jesus will be even more special once we learn how to truly listen.

Listen is the seventh spoke in the Spiritual Wheel of GOD (the Gifts of Development). God knows you first must listen and hear what He has to say in order to put in a good day's work. You must be able to hear Him.

In Lesson 7, I present the scriptures my prayer partner gave to me in the order the Holy Spirit had given to her. In this chapter, I give two testimonies: the first is of listening to God, and the second is my casual talks with Him in order to understand paranormal groups. Finally, I discuss the seven keys of *listen* that will help you understand your responsibility in serving God's people by listening and developing a relationship with the Holy Spirit.

Scriptures for Listen

The scriptures in this lesson provide examples on how to listen to the Holy Spirit. For example, the scriptures describe how the elders would not listen to Samuel. They wanted Samuel to appoint a king to them. Samuel delivered the message in the governance of the king. Other examples are about listening to the Word on observance that leads to blessings and the anointed bearer of glad tidings. The scriptures also speak of listening to God's voice and knowing that He is your God.

Therefore, all the elders of Israel assembled and went to Samuel at Ramah and said to him, "Now that you are old, and your example, appoint a king over us, like all the nations, to rule us." Samuel was displeased when they said, "Give us a king to rule us." But he prayed to the Lord. The Lord said: Listen to whatever the people say. You are not the one they are rejecting. They are rejecting me as their king. (1 Sam. 8:4–7)

Samuel delivered the message of the Lord in full to those who were asking him for a king. He told them: "The governance of the king who will rule you will be as follows: He will take your sons and assign them to his chariots and horses, and they will run before his chariot. He will appoint from among them his commanders of thousands and of hundreds. He will make them do his plowing and harvesting and produce his weapons of war and chariot. He will use your daughters as perfumers, cooks, and bakers. He will take your best fields, vineyards, and olive groves, and give them to his servants. He will tithe your crops and grape harvests to give to his officials and his servants. He will take your male and female slaves, as well as your best oxen and donkeys, and use them to do his work. He will also tithe your flocks. As for you, you will become his slaves. On that day you will cry out because of the king whom you have chosen, but the Lord will not answer you on that day. (1 Sam. 8:10–18)

The people, however, refused to listen to Samuel's warning and said, "No! There must be a king over us." . . . The Lord said: Listen to them! Appoint a king to rule over them. Then Samuel said to the people of Israel, "Return, each one of you, to your own city." (1 Samuel 8:19, 22)

Naaman, the army commander of the king of Aram, was highly esteemed and respected by his master, for through him the Lord had brought victory to Aram. But valiant as he was, the man was a leper. (2 Kings 5:1)

Naaman came with his horses and chariot and stopped at the door of Elisha's house. Elisha sent him the message: "Go and wash seven times in the Jordan, and your flesh will heal, and you will be clean. But Naaman went away angry, saying, "I thought that he would surely come out to me and stand there to call on the name of the Lord his God, and would move his hand over the place, and thus cure the leprous spot. Are not the rivers of Damascus, the Abana and the Pharpar, better than all the waters of Israel? Could I not wash in them and be cleansed?" With this, he turned about in anger and left. But his servants came up and reasoned with him: My father, if the prophet told you to do something extraordinary, would you not do it? All the more since he told you, "Wash, and be "clean?" (2 Kings 5:9–13)

So Naaman went down and plunged into the Jordan seven times, according to the word of the man of God. His flesh became again like the flesh of a little child, and he was clean. [15]He returned with his whole retinue to the man of God. On his arrival, he stood before him and said, "Now I know there is no God in all the earth, except in Israel. Please accept a gift from your servant." (2 Kings 5:14–15)

Every weapon fashioned against you shall fail; every tongue that brings you to trial you shall prove false. This is a lot of the servants of the Lord, their vindication from me—oracle of the Lord. (Is. 54:17)

Yet just as from the heavens the rain and snow come down and do not return there till, they have watered the earth, making it fertile and fruitful, Giving seed to the one who sows and bread to the one who eats· So shall my word be that goes forth from my mouth; it shall not return to me empty, but shall do what pleases me, achieving the end for which I sent it. (Is. 55:10–11)

Then you shall call, and the Lord will answer, you shall cry for help, and he will say: "Here I am!" If you remove the yoke from among you, the accuser, and malicious speech; If you lavish your food on the hungry and satisfy the afflicted; Then your light shall rise in the darkness, and your gloom shall become like midday; Then the Lord will guide you always and satisfy your thirst in parched places, will give strength to your bones and you shall be like a watered garden, like a flowing spring whose waters never fail. Your people shall rebuild the ancient ruins, the foundations from ages past you shall raise up;

repairer of the breach," they shall call you, restorer of ruined dwellings." (Is. 58:9–12)

If you refrain from trampling the Sabbath, from following your own pursuits on my holy day; if you call the Sabbath a delight, the Lord's holy day glorious; if you glorify it by not following your ways, seeking your own interests, or pursuing your own affairs— Then you shall delight in the Lord, and I will make you ride upon the heights of the earth; I will nourish you with the heritage of Jacob, your father, for the mouth of the Lord has spoken. (Is. 58:13–14)

The spirit of the Lord God is upon me, because the Lord has anointed me; He has sent me to bring good news to the afflicted, to bind up the brokenhearted, to proclaim liberty to the captives, release to the prisoners, to announce a year of favor from the Lord and a day of vindication by our God; to comfort all who mourn; to place on those who mourn in Zion a diadem instead of ashes, to give them oil of gladness instead of mourning, a glorious mantle instead of a faint spirit. They will be called oaks of justice, the planting of the Lord to show his glory. (Is. 61:1–3)

See, I am creating new heavens and a new earth; the former things shall not be remembered nor come to mind. Instead, shout for joy and be glad forever in what I am creating Jerusalem to be a joy and its people to be a delight; I will rejoice in Jerusalem and exult in my people. No longer shall the sound of weeping be heard there, or the sound of crying . . . (Is. 65:17–19)

I am coming to gather all nations and tongues; they shall come and see my glory. (Is. 66:18)

Before I formed you in the womb, I knew you, before you were born, I dedicated you, a prophet to the nations I appointed you . . . Then the Lord extended his hand and touched my mouth, saying to me, see, I place my words in your mouth! . . . But you prepare yourself; stand up and tell them all that I command you. Do not be terrified on account of them, or I will terrify you before them . . . They will fight against you, but not prevail over you, for I am with you to deliver you—oracle of the Lord. (Jer. 1:5, 9, 17, 19)

> This rather is what I commanded them: Listen to my voice; then I will be your God and you shall be my people. Walk exactly in the way I command you, so that you may prosper. (Jer. 7:23)
>
> The Lord is truly God, he is the living God, eternal King, before whose anger the earthquakes, whose wrath the nations cannot endure. (Jer. 10:10)
>
> Thus, I will fulfill the oath I swore to your ancestors, to give them a land flowing with milk and honey, the one you have today. "Amen, Lord," I answered. (Jer. 11:5)
>
> Blessed are those who trust in the Lord; the Lord will be their trust. They are like a tree planted besides the waters that stretches out its roots to the stream: it does not fear heat when it comes, its leaves stay green; in the year of drought, it shows no distress, but still produces fruit . . . I, the Lord, explore the mind and test the heart, giving to all according to their ways, according to the fruit of their deeds. (Jer. 17:7–8, 10)
>
> This word came to Jerimiah from the Lord: . . . Can I not do to you, house of Israel, as this potter has done? — oracle of the Lord. Indeed, like clay in the hand of the potter, so are you in my hand, house of Israel. (Jer. 18:1, 6)
>
> But the Lord is with me, like a mighty champion: my persecutors will stumble, they will not prevail. In their failure, they will be put to utter shame, to lasting, unforgettable confusion . . . Sing to the Lord, praise the Lord. For he has rescued the life of the poor from the power of the evildoers! (Jer. 20:11, 13)

Discussion of Scriptures for Listen

This is onc of my favorite lessons! Listening is something that I find to be fascinating. Jesus speaks to me every day and always has lots to say. Not a day goes by that I do not type what He tells me in less than two pages. He gives me encouragement in being obedient to His Word. He gives me assignments and messages to give to people who often do not know that I am going to give them a message.

Jesus is so good. When I first started listening to Jesus through the Listening Prayer in the mornings, He would communicate to me through thoughts. He would give me a phrase and waited until I typed it. He never goes too slow or too fast. He goes at a pace that is just right. Jesus would give me direction and instructions to His assignments. He would reveal things to me that made me wonder, *how am I so special to Him to allow me this great honor?* He says all God's people are special. All God's people can hear Him. So, when I came across Jerimiah 7:23, I was in awe of myself and what I felt. I felt light-hearted with the spirits of love, joy, and peace in God's grace. Wow!

> ". . . Listen to my voice; then I will be your God and you shall be my people. Walk exactly in the way I command you, so that you may prosper." (Jer. 7:23)

Which scriptures are significant to you and your personal experiences? Take a few minutes and reflect on how the scriptures relate in your life. Did a scripture stand out and resonate from within?

Lesson 7: Listen

In this section, I share four excerpts from my memoirs from when I spoke to Jesus in my morning prayers. Please note that my excerpts are taken from different years, but this just goes to show you how persistent our Lord is when He wants to send us messages! I also discuss two testimonies when the practice of listening was needed.

January 12, 2014
Sunday morning prayers

You will give Lesson 7 at the prayer meeting on Friday. You will be very pleased with it all. Some of the members need to understand that it is not them who are doing the work, but it is I, Jesus Christ. Lesson 7 will help them to understand how it works.

Lesson 7 is about listening. You must listen to the Holy Spirit. You must develop a relationship where you can hear the Holy Spirit talk to you. God will give you your assignments. He will tell you what to do. You will be able to talk to the Holy Spirit 24/7 and the Holy Spirit will answer you. You will share how you relate to Jesus, and how you pray every morning to receive your assignment and to hear what I have to say to you. You will tell them how long you pray in the mornings. They will be amazed at the time you take to pray every day. It will be the truth. [A prayer member] will have some questions. I will tell you what to say and do.

January 17, 2014
Friday morning prayers

You already know what to say in Lesson 7. People who receive spiritual gifts must learn how to listen to the Lord. They will learn the prayer of listening. Listening for their assignments. Listening to hear what God has to say to them in helping them in their purpose and ministry. One must know that they are only a vessel allowing God's work to work through them. God does all the work. Everything is going to work out. Keep going. Keep working. You will be pleased with the end results.

You have scriptures this morning. You will be very pleased. Your prayer partner will call to give them to you. You will read them before you go to the prayer meeting. You have a big night tonight. You will do a great job. You will follow My lead. You will be pleased with it all.

January 17, 2014
Friday evening prayer group meeting

Just as Jesus told me, I prepared for the prayer meeting. I read the scriptures Jesus had provided to me from my prayer partner. I was ready!

As usual, we sat around in a circle to pray and share. I waited for the other members to share what God had done for them, and then I spoke up.

"Lesson seven is about listening," I said. "It's so important to be able to listen to what the Holy Spirit has to say. You need to hear the Holy Spirit to receive your assignments. It is important to learn how to hear the Holy Spirit. God does all the work. We are the vessel that the Holy Spirit uses."

Everyone agreed. The air in the room felt lighter. Isn't it glorious to share God's message? Then I shared my two testimonies with the prayer group.

My Testimony 1: Listening to Jesus Christ

This testimony happened at the Life in the Spirit Seminar in 2009. It is appropriate to mention because it demonstrates how Jesus explained to me the importance of listening when He speaks to me.

October 2, 2009
Day 7 of the church seminar

"Good morning, dear Jesus. This morning I am here to listen to what you have to say."

Be still and listen, my child. You are the chosen one. You have lots of God's work to do. Sometimes it will not be easy, but you will be able to accomplish it. Many people need God's help. God will use you to help them. You will know when the time comes. You are beginning to know when I am speaking directly to you. You can discern. You have a gift that not everyone has, so use it wisely. The beginning and the end, Omega. You will know what that means later. For now, continue learning how to become closer to God, to Me. You will understand later what My plans are for you. You must keep the faith and continue on your path. Go now in peace.

I realize now how important it is to listen to what God has to say. For some, it will be Jesus talking directly to them, and for others, it will be the Holy Spirit. The power of the Listening Prayer is so important, which is why we should record what God is telling us during the Listening Prayer.

The Listening Prayer is when you pray and ask the Holy Spirit to speak to you, and you listen only to what He has to say. We can receive assignments, answers to our prayers, and anything God wants to reveal to us (see Lesson 1, Key 2, to learn how to hear the Holy Spirit every day).

My Testimony 2: Understanding Paranormal Groups

In my second testimony, Jesus demonstrated how listening to Him can give us assignments and valuable information in what I call "casual talks." Casual talk is when I talk to Jesus and He talks to me. You have to be able to hear the Holy Spirit in order to be able to do God's work.

December 15, 2009
Tuesday morning prayers

Jesus instructed me to watch a TV series about paranormal groups that would go to people's homes to help them with the evil activities in their homes. I had a question about the paranormal groups and their ability to get rid of evil. Whenever, I would ask Jesus a question, He would already know the question. Oftentimes I just have to ask if I can ask a question and He will answer me.

"Dear Jesus, may I ask you a question?" [Do paranormal groups help to drive out demons?]

Yes. The paranormal groups do help to drive out demons. They are not led by Me the way you are led. They do pray to Me and ask for my help. The people who are possessed pray for help, and I send them help through the paranormal team. You drive out demons differently. Your power is far more powerful than theirs. You will often be called upon to help them with the demons that are really stubborn. Your power can drive out any demon, any evil. These paranormal activities are real. From time to time, you will work with paranormal teams. They will hear about you and will contact you for advice in stubborn instances. I will direct you about what to do. No evil can touch you. You are too powerful in the Word. Go now. Go in peace. God has spoken.

I learned that there are a lot of paranormal activities going on in this world and are well documented. People don't go around talking about it until it happens to them and they need help. The more we understand what is happening, the better we can confront and get rid of the evil around us. Through Jesus Christ we can do all things. Thank you, Jesus, for your love and kindness in providing the seven keys of listening, a way of hearing what you have to say.

The Seven Keys for Listen

Lesson 7, "Listen," helps us to understand our responsibility in serving God's people by listening to the Word of God. All of this is possible through developing a relationship with the Holy Spirit.

The seven keys are *listen, learn, relationship, prayer, assignment, purpose,* and *the art of listening.*

1. **Listen** to the Holy Spirit.
2. **Learn**: People who receive spiritual gifts must learn how to listen to the Holy Spirit.
3. **Relationship**: Develop a relationship where you can hear the Holy Spirit talk to you.
4. **Prayer**: Learn the prayer of listening.
5. **Assignment**: Be able to listen for your assignments.
6. **Purpose**: Listen to hear what God has to say to you in helping you with your purpose and ministry.
7. **The Art of Listening:** Know that you cannot perform your spiritual gifts without the art of listening to God.

Key 1: Listen

One of the most important things you must do with your anointing is to acknowledge that you have to listen to the Holy Spirit. You must hear Him to do God's work. Your spiritual gifts work hand in hand with listening to the Holy Spirit. There are people who pray for their spiritual gifts every day not knowing that they need to hear the Holy Spirit at will, not just every now and then. You must strategically learn how to hear the Holy Spirit within you every day.

For more information about listening, refer to my morning and evening prayers throughout the book. That is a great representation of how Jesus speaks to me because I listen to Him. It is with my communicating with Jesus that I wrote this book and received the ten lessons He provided for it. In order to implement your anointing, you must be able to hear the Holy Spirit communicate with you (see the Listening Prayer in Chapter 1, Key 2).

You must know you need to hear the Holy Spirit every day in order for the Holy Spirit to teach and guide you.

> The Advocate, the Holy Spirit that the Father will send in my name—he will teach you everything and remind you of all that [I] told you. (John 14:26)

Key 2: Learn

You have to learn how to listen to the Holy Spirit if you do not know how to listen. You must be able to hear the Holy Spirit daily. People who receive spiritual gifts must learn how to listen to the Holy Spirit. Practice the Listening Prayer and wait to hear the Holy Spirit speak to you. Find a quiet place where you will be uninterrupted. You should try to find a time every day devoted to listening to the Holy Spirit. Sit quietly and ask the Holy Spirit to speak to you. Then record everything the Holy Spirit says. Don't try to understand it, just record what the Holy Spirit says. After the Holy Spirit finishes speaking to you, read what you wrote for comprehension.

For as long as I can remember, I could hear the Lord speaking to me every now and then, nothing consistent like a daily routine. Sometimes my gut feeling would warn me, and I would either listen to it or ignore it if I wanted to do it anyway. When I would ignore it, I would sometimes say to myself, "I had a feeling I should not have done that."

It was not until I took the Life in the Spirit Seminar at my church that I learned how to hear Jesus speak to me on a regular daily basis. We would have daily readings from the seminar that I would read in the mornings. Jesus just started talking to me through thoughts and gave me instructions and assignments like the ones you have read in this book. It is such a wonderful feeling being able to talk with God directly, living in the Spirit. Allowing Jesus to guide and lead me. Thank you, Jesus, thank you.

> But when he comes, the Spirit of truth, he will guide you to all truth. He will not speak on his own, but he will speak what he hears, and will declare to you the things that are coming. (John 16:13)

Key 3: Relationship

Learning how to listen to the Holy Spirit is like riding a bike. It can take a while to learn how to ride a bike to be in a marathon race. You train and practice for a long time to get into shape to endure the race. You have to do the same when listening to the Holy Spirit. The more you practice, the more you learn how to hear the Holy Spirit. You will learn how to get to that place where you can hear the Holy Spirit at any place or time, day, or night. It is establishing a relationship with the Holy Spirit.

I learned how to hear Jesus speak to me on a daily basis at that church seminar. I could communicate to Him directly spiritually. I started having a real relationship with Him like having a relationship with someone here on earth. I had a beautiful experience with Jesus.

In my memoir, I wrote on October 3, 2009:

"I called my spiritual partner, my sister. I told her what the Lord told me about speaking in tongues. Little did I know that she spoke in tongues. She had to refresh my memory. When we went to a healing Mass, I remembered she spoke in tongues. She asked Jesus for the gift. And then suddenly while we were talking, she started speaking in tongues. It was so beautiful. It was almost like she was singing. Her speaking in tongues filled me up until I started shouting, 'Alleluia, yes Jesus, I will be obedient.' I just shouted out at the top of my voice praising Him and chanting alleluia repeatedly and that I would be obedient. It seemed like I was given instructions on a deeper level than human. As if Jesus gave me instructions directly to my soul by passing the human aspects of my body. It was so beautiful."

What I learned was that my sister also has special gifts, reads the Bible and is holy. A scripture came to me after reading my excerpt with Jesus saying, "What I say to you, I say to all (Mark 13:37)." We all can have a relationship with Jesus. The Life in the Spirit Seminar taught me how to live in the spirit with Jesus Christ and to have a real spiritual relationship in speaking and communicating directly with Him. Living in the spirit. You can do it too.

> If the spirit of the one who raised Jesus from the dead dwells in you, the one who raised Christ from the dead will give life to your mortal bodies also, through his Spirit that dwells in you. (Rom. 8:11)

Key 4: Prayer

Prayer is speaking freely to God. There are different ways of praying, such as by adoration, petition, contrition, praise, thanksgiving, etc. I like practicing the Listening Prayer, where you ask the Holy Spirit to speak to you, and it is the Holy Spirit that does all of the talking. You record what the Holy Spirit tells you and read it afterwards for comprehension.

My memoirs of my morning prayers in this book are listening prayers. You must learn the prayer of listening. Pray the Listening Prayer to God every day. For instance, "Good morning, Holy Spirit. Do you have anything to say?" Then wait to listen to what He has to say. Open up your heart and listen and record what you hear.

> With all prayer and supplication, pray at every opportunity in the Spirit. To that end, be watchful with all perseverance and supplication for all the holy ones . . . (Eph. 6:18)
>
> Pray without ceasing. (1 Thess. 5:17)

Key 5: Assignment

You can receive assignments through listening to the Holy Spirit among other things the Holy Spirit may say to you. The Holy Spirit works through you. It is not I, but the Father above. Jesus Christ does all the work. You are the vessel that the Holy Spirit uses to help save God's people. You are assigned to do God's work. It is not your decision but God's decision. When people ask you to help them, you must first ask the Holy Spirit to see if it is your assignment to do.

All assignments may not be given to you in your listening prayers. Assignments can be given at any time of the day or night and in different ways. You can receive them in dreams, or you may get a thought in your head that you just know you need to give someone a message even if you don't know the person.

For example, you are attending a conference and are standing in the lobby mingling among the attendees waiting to enter the conference room. You notice a woman standing across from you. You get this feeling that you have a message for her. You walk over and say, "Excuse me, but I feel I have a message for you. May I give it to you?" She says yes, and you proceed with the message. More than likely you may never see that person again.

An assignment doesn't mean that it has to be preplanned. It can be instantaneous at that very moment. The Holy Spirit will determine how and when He will deliver messages to you. Just be receptive to receive them.

> And the one who searches hearts knows what is the intention of the Spirit, because it intercedes for the holy ones according to God's will. (Rom. 8:27)

Key 6: Purpose

As you learn to listen to God, you will be told about your purpose and ministry. He will guide you through to your purpose and ministry. (Ministry is discussed in Lesson 9.)

What is your spiritual purpose? How are you going to help God's children save their souls? How does God know what type of spiritual gifts to give you? Clearly, they match your purpose and ministry. Jesus told me everyone comes with a blueprint here on Earth, predestined to a certain extent that you may know the end results. It is how you get there is where the work lies. I really did not know what I would be doing until I took the Life in the Spirit Seminar. It changed my life entirely. Who would think I would be sitting here writing this book and having all these spiritual experiences? It's amazing.

God will reveal your purpose and ministry. It will happen in various times of your lives. Some know early in life, while others find out later in life. I started learning later in life. I am an educator, and my purpose is helping to save souls through my books, spiritual teaching, spiritual readings, prophecy, healing, and casting out demons.

> This was according to the eternal purpose that he accomplished in Christ Jesus our Lord. (Eph. 3:11)
>
> We know that all things work for good for those who love God, who are called according to his purpose. (Rom. 8:28)

Key 7: The Art of Listening

You cannot perform your spiritual gifts without the art of listening to God. God must tell you what to do. Do you hear the Holy Spirit audibly, through thought, visions and/or telepathically? Your style of listening can be different from others. You must learn how to hear Him, and with practice, you will learn how to hear Him every day.

Listening is a skill. When you are listening to the Lord, you do not try to understand what He is saying. You are writing it down to get the message on paper. When you finish, you read for comprehension. If you have questions, you ask the Holy Spirit and wait for an answer.

> Do you not know that your body is a temple of the Holy Spirit within you, whom you have from God, and that you are not your own? For you have been purchased at a price. Therefore, glorify God in your body. (1 Cor.6:19–20)
>
> And I will ask the Father, and he will give you another Advocate to be with you always, the Spirit of truth, which the world cannot accept, because it neither sees nor knows it. But you know it, because it remains with you, and will be in you. (John 14: 16–17)

Summary

Lesson 7, "Listening," is the seventh spoke of the Spiritual Wheel of GOD (the Gifts of Development). The seven keys are *listen, learn, relationship, prayer, assignments, purpose,* and *the art of listening.*

You must listen to the Holy Spirit. People who receive spiritual gift(s) must learn how to listen to the Holy Spirit. You must develop a relationship where you can hear the Holy Spirit talk to you 24/7. You must learn the prayer of listening. You must be able to listen for your assignment. Listen to hear what God has to say to you about your purpose and ministry. Know that you cannot perform your spiritual gifts without the art of listening to God. Your spiritual gift(s) and listening to the Holy Spirit every day go hand in hand together. To listen you have to be obedient to the Lord's words that you heard.

Chapter 8
Lesson 8: Obedience

"If you obey him and carry out all I tell you, I will be an enemy to your enemies and a foe to your foes." ~Exodus 23:22

Be consistent with obeying the Holy Spirit in what He tells you to do. You cannot perform your spiritual gift well without obedience. You will perform your gift when the Holy Spirit tells you to, not when you want to. Let God's will be done and on His time.

Obedience is the eighth spoke in the Spiritual Wheel of GOD (the Gifts of Development). If you are one of the millions of families in the United States who owns a pet, you are familiar with the concept of obedience. Our loveable, fluffy friends depend on us to feed them, clean up after them, and walk them. And we don't mind doing it! We love our family dogs and cats (and lizards and hamsters). When they listen—when they are obedient—we love them even more.

We are not domesticated, fluffy animals, but we are God's children, and He wants us to be obedient. He wants us to listen and then obey His command in performing our spiritual gift(s).

In Lesson 8, I discuss the scriptures that were given to me by my prayer partner. I also share a prayer member's testimony who wanted to heal a four-year-old boy who was dying of cancer. Separate from the prayer group meeting, I also share my testimony on when I was obedient to Jesus at a national convention as I waited for someone to come up to me who did not know I had a message for them. Finally, I discuss the seven keys of obedience that show you how you need to be obedient to God in order to let God's will be done.

Scriptures for Obedience

The scriptures for this chapter are on obedience in completing assignments. Jesus appointed twelve apostles, which the scriptures mention the mission of the twelve, and healing of the deaf. The scriptures go on to say that all things are possible for God. You must have faith to be obedient. Do not worry beforehand what to say. Just say whatever will be given to you at that hour by God.

> He appointed twelve [whom he also named apostles]
> that they might be with him and he might send them forth

to preach and to have authority to drive out demons . . . (Mar 3:14–15)

The scribes who had come from Jerusalem said, "He is possessed by Beelzebub," and "By the prince of demons he drives out demons." (Mark 3:22)

Summoning them, he begins to speak to them in parables, "How can Satan drive out Satan? . . . And if Satan has risen up against himself and is divided, he cannot stand that is the end of him . . . But whoever blasphemes against the Holy Spirit will never have forgiveness but is guilty of an everlasting sin." (Mark 3: 23, 26, 29)

And some seed fell on rich soil and produced fruit. It came up and grew and yielded thirty, sixty, and a hundredfold" . . . (Mark 4:8)

He answered them, "The mystery of the kingdom of God has been granted to you. But to those outside everything comes in parables, so that 'they may look and see but not perceive, and hear and listen but not understand, in order that they may not be converted and be forgiven." . . . The sower sows the word . . . But those sown on rich soil are the ones who hear the word and accept it and bear fruit thirty and sixty and hundredfold. (Mark 4:12, 14, 20)

For there is nothing hidden except to be made visible; nothing is secret except to come to light . . . He also told them, "Take care what you hear. The measure with which you measure will be measured out to you, and still more will be given to you." (Mark 4:22, 24)

When he got out of the boat, at once a man from the tombs who had an unclean spirit met him. The man had been dwelling among the tombs, and no one could restrain him any longer, even with a chain. In fact, he had frequently been bound with shackles and chains, but the chains had been pulled apart by him and the shackles smashed, and no one was strong enough to subdue him. Night and day among the tombs and on the hillsides, he was always crying out and bruising himself with stones. (Mark 5:2–5)

Catching sight of God from a distance, he ran up and prostrated himself before him, crying out in a loud voice, "What have you to do with me, Jesus, son of the Most High God? I adjure you by God, do not torment me!" (He had been saying to him, "Unclean spirit, come out of the man!") He asked him, "What is your name?" He replied, "Legion is my name. There are many of us. (Mark 5:6–9)

And he pleaded earnestly with him not to drive them away from that territory. Now a large herd of swine was feeding there on the hillside. And they pleaded with him, "Send us into the swine. Let us enter them." And he let them, and the unclean spirits came out and entered the swine. The heard of about two thousand rushed down a steep bank into the sea, where they were drowned. (Mark 5:10–13)

As they approached God, they caught sight of the man who had been possessed by Legion, sitting there clothed and in his right mind. And they were seized with fear. (Mark 5:15)

There was a woman afflicted with hemorrhages for twelve years. She had suffered greatly at the hands of many doctors and had spent all that she had. Yet she was not helped but only grew worse. She had heard about Jesus and came up behind him in the crowd and touched his cloak. She said, "If I but touch his clothes, I shall be cured. Immediately her flow of blood dried up. She felt in her body that she was healed of her affliction. (Mark 5:25–29)

Jesus, aware at once that power had gone out from him, turned around in the crowd and asked, "Who has touched my clothes?" . . . He said to her, "Daughter, your faith has saved you. Go in peace and be cured of your affliction . . . . Disregarding the message that was reported, God said to the synagogue official. "Do not be afraid; just have faith." (Mark 5: 30, 34, 36)

He was amazed at their lack of faith. *The mission of the twelve.* He went around to the villages in the vicinity teaching . . . So, they went off and preached repentance. They drove out many demons, and they anointed with oil many who were sick and cured them. (Mark 6:6, 12, 13)

Soon a woman whose daughter had an unclean spirit heard about him. She came and fell at his feet. The woman was a Greek, a Syrophoenician by birth, and she begged him to drive the demon out of her daughter. (Mark 7:25–26)

He said to her, "Let the children be fed first. For it is not right to take the food of children and throw it to the dogs. She replied and said to him, "Lord, even the dogs under the table eat the children's scraps. Then he said to her, "For saying this, you may go. The demon has gone out of your daughter." When the woman went home, she found the child lying in bed and the demon gone. (Mark 7:27–30)

And people brought to him a deaf man who had a speech impediment and begged him to lay his hand on him. He took him off by himself away from the crowd. He put his finger into the man's ears and, spitting, touched his tongue; then he looked up to heaven and groaned, and said to him, "Ephphatha!" (that is, "Be opened!") and [immediately] the man's ears were opened, his speech impediment was removed, and he spoke plainly. (Mark 7:32–35)

What profit is there for one to gain the whole world and forfeit his life? (Mark 8:36)

After six days God took Peter, James, and John and led them up a high mountain apart by themselves. And he was transfigured before them, and his clothes became dazzling white, such as no fuller on earth could bleach them. Then Elijah appeared to them along with Moses, and they were conversing with God . . . Then a cloud came, casting a shadow over them; then from the cloud came a voice, "This is my beloved Son. Listen to him" . . . (Mark 9:2–4, 7)

Someone from the crowd answered him, "Teacher, I have brought to you my son possessed by a mute spirit. Wherever it seizes him, it throws him down; he foams at the mouth, grinds his teeth, and becomes rigid. I asked your disciples to drive it out, but they were unable to do so." He said to them in reply, "O faithless generation, how long will I endure you? Bring him to me." They brought the boy to him. And when he saw him, the spirit immediately threw the boy into convulsions. As he fell to the ground, he began to roll around and foam at the mouth. Then he questioned his father, "How long has this been happening to him?" He replied, "Since childhood. It has often thrown him into fire and into water to kill him. But if you can do anything, have compassion on us and help us." Jesus said to him. "If you can! Everything is possible to one who has faith." Then the boy's father cries out, "I do believe, help my unbelief." Jesus, on seeing a crowd rapidly gathering, rebuked the unclean spirit and said to it, "Mute and deaf spirit, I command you: come out of him and never enter him again!" Shouting and throwing the boy into convulsions, it came out. He became like a corpse, which caused many to say, "He is dead!" But God took him by the hand, raised him, and he stood up. When he entered the house, his disciples asked him in private, "Why could we not drive it out?" He said to them, "This kind can only come out through prayer." (Mark 9:17–29)

"For whoever is not against us is for us. Anyone who gives you a cup of water to drink because you belong to God, Amen. I say to you, will surely not lose his reward." (Mark 9: 40–41)

Therefore, what God has joined together; no human being must separate. (Mark 10:9)

Jesus looked at them and said, "For human beings it is impossible, but not for God. All things are possible for God." (Mark 10:27)

Jesus said to them in reply, "Have faith in God." Amen, I say to you, whoever says to this mountain, 'Be lifted up and thrown into the sea,' and does not doubt in his heart but believes that what he says will happen, it shall be done for him. Therefore, I tell you, all that you ask for in prayer, believe that you will receive it and it shall be yours. When you stand to pray, forgive anyone against whom you have a grievance, so that your heavenly Father may in turn forgive you your transgressions." (Mark 11:22–25)

They were seeking to arrest him, but they feared the crowd, for they realized that he had addressed the parable to them. So, they left him and went away. (Mark 12:12)

God replied, "The first is this: 'Hear, O Israel! The Lord our God is Lord alone! You shall love the Lord your God with all your heart, with all your soul, with all your strength.' The second is this: 'You shall love your neighbor as yourself.' There is no other commandment greater than these." (Mark 12:29–31)

> "When they lead you away and hand you over, do not worry beforehand about what you are to say. But say whatever will be given to you at that hour. For it will not be you who are speaking but the Holy Spirit." (Mark 13:11)
>
> What I say to you, I say to all: 'Watch'!'" (Mark 13:37)

Discussion of Scriptures for Obedience

What I appreciate about these scriptures is the disciples' obedience when they accompanied Jesus. They were obedient to go out and preach the Word on their own.

Several scriptures stood out to me: Mark 6:6, 12, Mark 13:37, and Mark 11:22. The disciples were sent out to teach, preach repentance, drive out demons, and heal the sick. Jesus says, "What I say to you, I say to all. Watch!"

I get it. Jesus has given me my anointing by sending me out to teach, to spread the good news, to heal, and to cast out demons. I must have faith and be obedient to God's words and His assignments.

Which scriptures are significant to you and your personal experiences? Take a few minutes and reflect on how the scriptures relate in your life. Did a scripture stand out and resonate from within?

Lesson 8: Obedience

In this section, I share excerpts from my memoirs, as well as my sharing Jesus' message to my prayer group. I also share a prayer member's testimony of wanting to heal a child who had cancer, and my own testimony on obedience.

January 23, 2014
Thursday morning prayers

You will give Lesson 8 tomorrow. As you work with people, you can see how your book is needed for people to understand how to use their gifts. You can see how people are somewhat confused. You will tell the story about the four-year-old cancer patient who was dying. You will tell how the prayer group member thought he was going to heal the child, and how he was devastated when he didn't heal him. He thought he was given the power to healing rather than allowing his body to be a vessel for God to do the healing. Many will learn a lesson from that.

Lesson 8 is on obedience. They must be obedient to the Word. After they listen to the Holy Spirit, they must then be obedient to implement His Word. They must do what they are told to do whether they like it or not, or feel like it, or are embarrassed. Your ministry is a lifetime commitment of work and obedience. These lessons are in a particular order on how to experience spiritual awakening. This book will be read by many. All those who are going to have a spiritual awakening should read this book. Those who are experiencing a spiritual awakening should read this book. Those who have been in the spiritual awakening should read this book. It will help them to understand what is expected of them when they receive their gifts.

January 24, 2014
Friday morning prayers

You will go to the prayer meeting tonight. You will deliver messages, and you will cast out evil in a man that a prayer group member will bring to the meeting. He has had evil for a very long time. He has been praying to get rid of it. The time has come. You will be very pleased with it all. The man will act very strange in the meeting. He will move around in demonic ways. The members will feel uncomfortable until they see you there. You will walk in, and he will stop the demonic movements. Everyone there will know you have an effect on him. You will walk in and sit down. The man will say in a little boy's voice, "Can you help me? I've been trapped inside my own body for years." You will say, "Do you want to get rid of it?" He will say, "Yes."

You will ask for the children to leave the room. The man will start acting weird again. You will have the members pray for the deliverance of the man while you cast the demon out. You will tell them, "Do not be afraid. God is right here in the room. You are protected. However, if you feel uncomfortable you may leave now." No one will leave. You will be fierce with him. You will speak guttural tongues like you never have before. You will win. When you finish, the evil will be gone. You will see the evil for the first time, and you will see it leave his body.

You will write about it. It will be amazing to see it and be a part of the experience. You will tell the man, "It is gone, and it will never return." When he thanks you, you will say for everyone to hear, "It is not I, but the Father above. God did all the work." The prayer leader will say, "Bring in the children and let us pray."

You will be pleased. The man will weep in front of everyone. He will say to everyone, "It is gone. I lived with evil for years." You will walk up to him and comfort him. You will tell him, "I believe you. Yes, it is gone." When you give Lesson 8, the members will listen. They know you are a very holy woman. You will be the talk of the parish. They even got a chance to be involved with the exorcism. Everyone will be pleased that it is gone.

[This exorcism has not yet happened.]

January 24, 2014
Friday evening prayer group meeting

After the prayer members shared their experiences, the theme of the night became clear: obedience. Prayer members expressed their experience with obedience in their own special way. I mentioned to the group a scripture that came to my mind: "What I say to you, I say to all. Watch!" (Mark 13:37). We were all experiencing obedience. To perform our spiritual gift(s) effectively, we must be obedient to God. He uses us as a vessel and determines when we will use them.

January 25, 2014
Saturday morning prayers

You did a great job with the Lesson 8 on obedience. You saw how it all came together. It was a common thread throughout the whole night. The prayer leaders knew what you meant about Mark 13:37: "What I say to you, I say to all: Watch!" The co-prayer leader understood that obedience was the theme of the night. So, after the testimonies for the night, they were ready to hear the lesson on obedience with their own testimonies that they could relate to. You were pleased at the end of the night and so was everyone else. They now have a reason to come. They are beginning to get it as you speak to them about spiritual awakening. They will return to hear more.

My Testimony 1: Obedience

Prior to the prayer meeting, a prayer member came to me asking to confirm his spiritual gift of healing. I meditated for a minute and God confirmed that he was a healer. In the prayer meeting, he mentioned that another prayer member asked him to go to the home of a parent whose four-year-old son had cancer. When the prayer member went to the boy's home, his parents asked if the prayer member would pray over the boy, the house, and in the boy's room. The boy did not want him to pray in his room or over him. The prayer member said he did it anyway. He then left the home and found out later the boy died that night.

The prayer member who tried to heal the boy was devastated. He felt that he was a healer, so he questioned why he wasn't able to heal the four-year-old boy with cancer. There was a prayer group discussion explaining that the Holy Spirit does all the work. The prayer member is only the vessel that the Holy Spirit uses. The Holy Spirit gives you assignments to perform. If it is not your assignment, you will not be able to perform the healing. You must be obedient and perform only the assignments that are given to you.

In the case of the four-year-old boy, it was time for him to cross over. Even the little boy knew it was time. That is why he didn't want him to come into his room nor pray over him. There was nothing the healer could do to heal the boy without God's divine intervention. There wasn't anything wrong with the healer; it just wasn't his assignment to heal him. It was just time for the little four-year-old boy to cross over.

A discussion followed afterwards. What the member didn't understand was that he didn't do the healing. God uses your body as a vessel to heal who He wants healed. It was up to God to determine if He wanted the boy to live. In that instance, God chose not to heal him. The child knew it was time. Another prayer member was there to soothe and help the parents along with the healer.

When the member was asked to come and pray over the boy for healing, he should have prayed to God and waited for the answer of what he should do. The prayer member took it upon himself to pray over the boy even though the boy didn't want that. But as you know, everything is God's decision to make.

My Testimony 2: Delivering a Message

Another example of obedience came when I was given an assignment to deliver a message to a colleague who was depressed. We were at a national conference, and she didn't know that I was going to give her a message from God.

I knew I had to be obedient and wait for someone to come up to me. I also knew I had to have faith that I would know when the person approached me and be obedient to follow the instructions by the Lord as He would give them to me during the encounter with her.

March 15, 2013
National Conference

You will run into a woman today. She is going to be very depressed. She is just going to start talking to you. She is going to tell you her problems. I will tell you what to say and do. You will help her. She will feel better after talking to you.

After prayer, I dressed and went downstairs for breakfast and the first conference session of the day. I didn't know who the woman would be, but I was curious to find out.

As I was walking in the hotel lobby, I dropped my packet that had my room key cards. They fell out of the packet and I was trying to pick them up. I was able to pick up one of them, but I was having a hard time picking up the other. One woman whom I had spoken to earlier came over. "Do you need any help," she asked as she picked up the card for me.

We stood up at the same time. I thanked her and we introduced ourselves and made small talk.

"I didn't sleep well last night," she said. "I woke up with a minor migraine and have had it for several days now. Just overall I don't feel well." She then told me her childhood experience with God. She had never told anyone about it. I believe she felt safe telling me. We lived in different parts of the country, so we probably wouldn't see each other again or at least for a year until the next conference.

When she was a little girl, God spoke to her and forewarned her of a man who was going to try to kidnap her. God told her, "You must do three things all at the same time to be saved. One, you must snatch your hand away. Two, scream as loud as you can. And three, you must run as fast as you can."

She was twelve when it happened. A man had tried to kidnap her. She had left the metal gate open as she went down the street to visit with her friend. A black van was parked, and the side door slid open. As she was walking, a man grabbed at her but did not get a good grip. She remembered what God had told her. She snatched her arm away and turned around screaming and running as fast as she could. She had on a dress with black patent-leather shoes. Her dress was tied with a ribbon-like belt in the back, which came loose and was hanging down as she ran.

Her mother came out of the house first followed by the father. The gate was already opened, and her mother ran out to get her. She grabbed her daughter into her arms and took her into the house. The black van drove off and was never seen again. She was too scared to tell her parents that God already told her what to do. So, she held this secret in until now.

Keep in mind, I was at a national convention and a woman told me of her experience with God when she was a little girl. I realized for myself how people (adults and children) were experiencing supernatural things all over the country. Me and this woman lived in different states, so I knew for a fact that our encounter was no coincidence. God told me I would meet someone, just like He told her she would have an encounter with a man who would try to kidnap her.

Wow! God assigned me to talk to her. God knew she needed a woman to talk to. Thank you, Lord, for allowing me to be that woman, your vessel. God distributes His assignments and anointings as He so desires.

"Since that incident, I've been scared and afraid of men," she said. "I don't know what my purpose is here on Earth."

I said, "You have been having migraines and nightmares since the incident occurred?"

"Yes, I have," she responded.

I told her, "God wants you to know that you need not be afraid anymore." Then God explained how evil preys on fear. The stronger the fear, the more energy you give to evil. God told me to tell her she did not need to be afraid anymore. She was God's child, and she was protected. God would protect her. He would take care of her.

"Do you believe in God?" I asked.

She nodded. "Yes."

I explained to her that we all come on this earth to serve God. "You were saved when you were twelve because you have work to do in serving God. There are two ways to serve Him: you are either a minister on the pulpit, so to speak, or you are a minister among the people as one of the people," I said.

God told me to tell her that she was a minister among the people as one of the people. He told me to tell her to find a Christian church that she liked and to go to church on Sundays and get involved in the church in helping people. She agreed.

God then told me to ask her if I could pray over her, and she said yes with enthusiasm. When I began to pray tongues over her, she quickly pulled me over to the side next to the wall. She bent her head down while I prayed tongues over her. I touched her head in prayer.

When I finished, Jesus told me to remind her that anytime she had a nightmare or was afraid, she should rebuke it in the name of Jesus Christ, and it would go away. I also reminded her that God would protect her. She didn't need to be afraid anymore. No harm would come to her. God would also provide for her and take care of her.

She thanked me and told me she was going to find her colleagues. We said our goodbyes.

There were so many people at the convention that I didn't get a chance to see her again or to say goodbye at the end of the conference. But her story stuck with me. The day before I had sat at her table, both of us with our respective colleagues. I never would have known what she had gone through when she was twelve, or how much that one incident had affected her life into adulthood.

I realized how many people could be hurting inside and you wouldn't know by outside appearances. Thank you, Jesus, for allowing me to be the vessel to help that woman get into her ministry in helping people through a Christian church.

The Seven Keys for Obedience

Lesson 8, "Obedience," discusses how God wants us to be obedient, and that we need to be consistent with obeying the Holy Spirit in what He tells us to do.

The seven keys are *consistency, timing, messages, obligation, feelings, cost,* and *responsibility.*

1. **Consistency**: Be consistent with obeying the Holy Spirit in what He tells you to do.
2. **Timing**: Timing is everything. You do not do it when you want to, but when you are told to.
3. **Messages**: Do not worry how things turn out or how a person accepts the message.
4. **Obligation**: After you listen to the Holy Spirit, you have an obligation to be obedient to His Word.
5. **Feelings**: Do what you are told whether you like it or not, whether you are embarrassed or not, or whether you are confused with the assignment.
6. **Cost**: Doing what you are told at all costs is not an easy thing to do.
7. **Responsibility**: It is your responsibility and duty to obey the Word of God.

Key 1: Consistency

Always do what you are told to do. Be consistent with obeying the Holy Spirit. You are to do your tasks on a regular basis whether you are in the mood to do it or not. Consistency is the key. Just keep going. Keep on doing what you are called to do.

One of the things that you must do is to be consistent in praying to the Holy Spirit every day, to be consistent in hearing what the Holy Spirit has to say, and to be consistent in doing what the Holy Spirit wants you to do. In other words, you have to be consistent in being obedient to what God wants for you and your anointing.

I get up early in the morning, and the first thing I do is pray my Listening Prayer where I listen and record what the Lord has to say. I always start my day in prayer. There were times I would feel sleepy or just did not feel like praying, but I prayed anyway. On those days, I ask the Lord to give me strength to pray and hear His Word. I also have to listen to the assignments He gives me in my morning prayer or throughout the day. I must be consistent to do what I am told to do, and that is to be obedient.

> Remind them to be under control of magistrates and authorities, to be obedient, to be open to every good enterprise. (Titus 3:1)

Key 2: Timing

Timing is everything. You are not on your own timeline; you are on God's timeline. Things must synchronize. Everything must fall into place. If you are supposed to meet someone at a certain time and you don't take it seriously to get there on time, you very well may miss the person you were supposed to meet. Take your anointing seriously.

When I receive instructions to attend church service at eight o'clock in the mornings during the week, or on Sundays at different times, I went. I was told to go at a certain time, and I obeyed.

Sometimes I will be somewhere—shopping, with friends, etc.—and I receive a message from God to tell someone a message. One time a woman walked up to me complaining of her shoulder when I was to heal her. If I did not go to the event, I would not have been able to be used as a vessel to heal her. I had a message for a woman who did not know I had a message for at a conference. If I had not gone downstairs to the conference meeting when I did, I would have missed her and would not have been able to be the vessel to deliver the message. Timing is important. You are not on your time but God's time.

> "Why do you call me, 'Lord, Lord,' but not do what I command? I will show you what someone is like who comes to me, listens to my words, and act on them." (Luke 6:46–47)
>
> You are my friends if you do what I command you. (John 15:14)

Key 3: Messages

You are responsible to deliver a message or perform a certain thing. Don't worry about how things turn out or how a person accepts the message. You are responsible to be obedient and do it regardless of what the outcome may be. When you deliver the message and/or performed your assignment, you have done your job. The outcome or the way the person receives the message is their responsibility not yours.

When I first started delivering messages to members in the charismatic prayer group meetings, I was worried about what the members would think of me. Sometimes they would even ask me if it were their messages or not. Jesus told me not to worry about how the person receiving the message accepts the messages. Those who pray to Him know if it is their message. If they are in question, they are to pray to Him for guidance. I am not to explain the message to them. It is not my message; it is God's message. I am just the vessel. God will confirm their message to them.

> "Not everyone who says Lord, Lord will enter the kingdom of heaven, but only the one who does the will of My Father." (Matt. 7:21)
>
> But Peter and the apostles said in reply, "We must obey God rather than men . . ." (Acts 5:29)

Key 4: Obligation

You must be obedient to God's Word. In doing so, you have an obligation to perform the spiritual gifts as the Holy Spirit requires of you. We do not get to pick and choose which assignments we want to perform.

For example, in casting out the demons in the three women in the charismatic prayer group [see Lesson 10], I really was uncomfortable and did not want to do it. What made me continue was that I knew I had to be obedient, and I had an obligation to do so. I do not get to pick and choose what I want to do with my anointing and neither do you.

Now please keep in mind that not all assignments are hard to do. Some you will be pleased in helping to save souls.

> . . . in the foreknowledge of God, the Father, through sanctification by the Spirit, for obedience and sprinkling with the blood of Jesus Christ: may grace and peace be yours in abundance. (1 Peter 1:2)

Key 5: Feelings

Do as you are told whether you like it or not, whether it embarrasses you, or whether you are confused about the assignment. It is not for you to judge how you deliver your messages or perform your gift. You are to be obedient to the Word. Sometimes you are tested on whether you can perform your special gifts even when you may feel embarrassed or uncomfortable for whatever reasons.

> He replied, "Rather, blessed are those who hear the word of God and observe it." (Luke 11:28)

Key 6: Cost

Cost may refer to money. However, the phrase, "at all costs" doesn't necessarily have to do with money. It could be morals or beliefs. For example, a woman might stand up for what she believes in at all costs, even though it cost her to sever ties with a close friend.

Oftentimes we will be challenged to do some of the assignments we are requested to do. We may want to do other things, but we must obey. Doing what we are told to do, no matter what the cost may be, is not an easy thing to do, but you must have trust in the Lord.

> Be doers of the word and not hearers only, deluding yourselves. For if anyone is a hearer of the word and not a doer, he is like a man who looks at his own face in a mirror. He sees himself, then goes off and promptly forgets what he looked like. But the one who peers into the perfect law of freedom and preservers and is not a hearer who forgets but a doer who acts, such one shall be blessed in what he does. (James 1:22–25)

Key 7: Responsibility

We are responsible to perform our assignments in a timely manner. Obedience is crucial to your anointing. Your special spiritual gifts are your responsibility and duty to perform exactly when you are given the assignment. Obey the Word of God.

> Do you not know if you present yourselves to someone as obedient slaves, you are slaves of one you obey, either of sin, which leads to death, or of obedience, which leads to righteousness? But thanks to God that, although you were once slaves to sin, you have become obedient from the heart to the pattern of teaching to which you were entrusted. (Rom. 6:16–17)

Summary

Lesson 8, "Obedience," is the eighth spoke of the Spiritual Wheel of GOD (the Gifts of Development). The seven keys in this lesson are *consistency, timing, messages, obligation, feelings, cost,* and *responsibility.*

Be consistent with obeying the Holy Spirit in what He tells you to do. Always do what you are told. Timing is everything. You are on God's timeline, not your own. Do not worry about how things turn out or how a person accepts the message.

After you listen to the Holy Spirit, you must be obedient to His Word. You will not be able to perform your anointing very well without obedience. You must do as you are told whether you like or not. Doing what you are told at all costs is not an easy thing to do. It is your responsibility and duty to obey the Word of God.

Chapter 9
Lesson 9: Ministry

"Yet I consider life of no importance to me, if only I may finish my course and the ministry that I received from the Lord God, to bear witness to the gospel of God's grace." ~Acts 20:24

Everyone has a ministry on Earth. Your ministry is a lifetime commitment of work and obedience to God. The things you experience in life are getting you ready to do your ministry, the purpose of why you are here.

Ministry is the ninth spoke in the Spiritual Wheel of GOD (the Gifts of Development). God develops you into your ministry as you go about obeying His commands in performing your spiritual gift(s).

In Lesson 9, I provide the scriptures that were given to me by my prayer partner. I also share my testimony of my ministry that God has given to me. Finally, I discuss the seven keys that will help you understand your responsibility in serving God's people through your purpose and ministry here on Earth.

Scriptures for Ministry

The scriptures in this lesson are from the perspective of your ministry. The scriptures stated how the Twelve Apostles went out two by two. Jesus gave authority to the Apostles over unclean spirits and the anointing and healing of the sick. The mute spirit, praise of the Father, and privileges of discipleship are also scriptures in this lesson.

> He summoned the twelve and began to send them out two by two and gave them authority over unclean spirits . . . They drove out many demons, and they anointed with oil many who were sick and cured them. (Mark 6:7, 13)
>
> In their synagogue was a man with an unclean spirit; he cried out. "What have you to do with us, Jesus of Nazareth? Have you come to destroy us? I know who you are—the Holy one of God!" Jesus rebuked him and said, "Quiet! Come out of him!" The unclean spirit convulsed him and with a loud cry came out of him. All were amazed and asked one another, "What is this? A new teaching with

authority. He commands even the unclean spirits, and they obey him. His fame spread everywhere throughout the whole region of Galilee. (Mark 1:23–28)

The scribes who had come from Jerusalem said, "He is possessed by Beelzebub," and "by the prince of demons he drives out demons." summoning them, he began to speak to them in parables, "How can Satan drive out Satan? If a kingdom is divided against itself, that kingdom cannot stand. And if a house is divided against itself, that house will not be able to stand. And if Satan has risen up against himself and is divided, he cannot stand; that is the end of him. (Mark 3:22–26)

Someone from the crowd answered him, "Teacher, I have brought to you my son possessed by a mute spirit . . . It has often thrown him into fire and into water to kill him. But if you can do anything, have compassion on us and help us. Jesus said to him. "If you can!' Everything is possible to one who has faith." Then the boy's father cried out, "I do believe, help my unbelief!" Jesus on seeing a crowd rapidly gathering, rebuked the unclean spirit and said to it, "Mute and deaf spirit, I command you: 'Come out of him and never enter him again!'" Shouting and throwing the boy into convulsions, it came out. He became like a corpse, which caused many to say, "He is dead!" When he entered the house, his disciples asked him in private, "Why could we not drive it out?" He said to them, "This kind can only come out through prayer. (Mark 9:17, 22–26, 28–29)

The seventy [-two] returned rejoicing, and said, "Lord, even the demons are subject to us because of your name . . . Nevertheless, do not rejoice because the spirits are subject to you, but rejoice because your names are written in heaven." (Luke 10:17, 20)

At that very moment he rejoiced [in] the Holy Spirit and said, "I give you praise, Father Lord of heaven and earth, for although you have hidden these things from the wise and the learned, you have revealed them to the childlike. Yes, Father, such has been your gracious will." (Luke 10:21)

Turning to the disciples in private he said, "Blessed are the eyes that see what you see. For I say to you, many prophets and kings desired to see what you see, but did not see it, and to hear what you hear, but did not hear it. (Luke 10:23–24)

He replied, "Rather, blessed are those who hear the word of God and observe it." (Luke 11:28)

He was driving out a demon [that was] mute, and when the demon had gone out, the mute person spoke, and the crowds were amazed. Some of them said, "By the power of Beelzebub, the prince of demands, he drives out demons." . . . But he knew their thoughts and said to them, "Every Kingdom divided against itself will be laid waste and house will fall against house. And if Satan is divided against himself, how will his kingdom stand? For you say that it is by Beelzebub that I drive out demons. If I, then, drive out demons by Beelzebub, by whom do your own people drive them out? Therefore, they will be your judges. But if it is by the finger of God that [I] drive out demons, then the kingdom of God has come upon you. When a strong man fully armed guards his palace, his possessions are safe. (Luke 11:14–15, 17–21)

When an unclean spirit goes out of someone, it roams through the regions searching for rest but, finding none, it says, "I shall return to my home from which I came. But upon returning, it finds it swept clean and put in order. Then it goes and brings back seven other spirits more wicked than itself who move in and dwell there, and the last condition of that person is worse than the first." (Luke 11:24–26)

There is nothing concealed that will not be revealed, nor secret that will not be known. Therefore, whatever you have said in the darkness will be heard in the light, and what you have whispered behind closed doors will be proclaimed on the housetops. (Luke 12:2–3)

I tell you, my friends, do not be afraid of those who kill the body but after that can do no more. I shall show you whom to fear. Be afraid of the one who after killing has the power to cast into Gehenna; yes, I tell you, be afraid of that one. (Luke 12:4–5)

. . . and the servant who was ignorant of his master's will but acted in a way deserving of a severe beating shall be beaten only lightly. Much will be required of the person entrusted with much, and still more will be demanded of the person entrusted with more. (Luke 12:48)

Someone in the crowd said to him, "Teacher, tell my brother to share the inheritance with me." . . . All the nations of the world seek for these things, and you Father knows that you need them. (Luke 12:13, 30)

For everyone who exalts himself will be humbled, but the one who humbles himself will be exalted . . . blessed indeed will you be because of their inability to repay you. For you will be repaid at the resurrection of the righteous." (Luke 14:11, 14)

And when she does find it, she calls together her friends and neighbors and says to them, "Rejoice with me because I have found the coin that I lost." In just the same way, I tell you, there will be rejoicing among the angels of God over one sinner who repents. (Luke 15:9–10)

". . . who would gladly have eaten his fill of the scraps that fell from the rich man's table. Dogs even used to come and lick his sores." (Luke 16:21)

And he said, "What is impossible for human beings is possible for God." (Luke 18:27)

Discussion of Scriptures for Ministry

I love these scriptures because we can see an example of the disciples' ministry, which was demonstrated in several scriptures: Mark 6:7, 13, Luke 10:17, 20, and Luke 10:23–24.

The disciples' ministry was to go out two by two and teach, preach, heal, and cast out demons with the authority of Jesus Christ's name. They came back rejoicing they were able to cast out demons in the name of Jesus Christ. Jesus said, "do not rejoice because the spirits are subject to you," but "rejoice because your names are written in heaven."

I understand how thankful I am that I can see what I see and hear what I hear. I have such a special relationship with Jesus Christ. It is such an honor to be the vessel to write this book. Thank you, Jesus, thank you.

Which scriptures are significant to you and your personal experiences? Take a few minutes and reflect on how the scriptures relate in your life. Did a scripture stand out and resonate from within?

Lesson 9: Ministry

For this lesson, I will provide excerpts from my memoirs with Jesus and the messages He gave me during my morning prayers. I also share my testimony with my prayer group of the time when Jesus revealed to me that I was a prophet.

January 25, 2014
Saturday morning prayers

You are now going to prepare for Lesson 9, ministry. Everyone has a ministry. Their ministry has to do with their experiences in life. Some will be simple, and some will be more complicated . . . it doesn't matter what it is. What matters is that you accept your ministry and do it well. Remember, the Good News Seminar in the church showed people with their different ministries. Each one of you has your own ministry. Pray for it to be revealed to you.

January 30, 2014
Thursday morning prayers

Tomorrow will be a big day at the church. You will give the Lesson 9 on ministry. Ministry is a big one because it is what the special gifts is all about, doing your ministry to help God's people. It is going to work out great. You will be very pleased with it all. Some will already know your ministry. Others will not have a clue. You will start them to thinking about it. They are pleased to hear about learning about spiritual awakening. The gifts will start coming to them. Tomorrow night there will be a few who will speak tongues. It will encourage the group that they, too, have special gifts from God. I will tell you what to say and do.

January 31, 2014
Friday morning prayers

You are going places. You have learned how to tap into the universe. You will have a great time next week with the prayer group. You will watch them speak in tongues. They will be fascinated. They will listen to you about ministry. When you told them to think about their own ministry, they will think about it and will come back the next week with the questions pertaining to it. I will tell you what to say and do.

January 31, 2014
Friday evening prayer group meeting

At the prayer group meeting, we started with worship songs that usually last about thirty minutes. Sharing time came next. That was when I would introduce the lesson for the night. I talked about my ministry and how everyone has a ministry. I told them about how Jesus revealed my ministry to me.

My Testimony

Jesus reveals to me that I am a prophet and a teacher. He revealed this to me in my morning prayers on August 8, 2013, and on October 7, 2015.

August 8, 2013
Thursday prayers

You understand how to function in the spiritual world. You are doing what you are supposed to do. You are a prophet. That is what makes you stand out from the rest of them. You are all powerful. The others function in one way or another. You function in all of them [spiritual gifts] at any given time. That is what makes you so special. You know how all of them work.

October 7, 2015
Wednesday morning prayers

Your ministry is to teach my people how to perform their spiritual gifts. You will write books to teach many souls all over the world. They will read your books and learn a lot from them.

Your ministry as a prophet is to help people in their problems in coping with the flesh. You will help many save their souls.

As I was writing this book, I often wondered what was my ministry. I sort of knew because I was living it. It wasn't until Jesus revealed to me that I was to teach His people the spiritual gifts and how to use them that I knew it was my ministry. I knew I was a prophet because He told me many times and long ago. Now I know I am a prophet and a teacher. Jesus often says to me, "Everywhere you go, people want to know who you are, so you tell them. You are a prophet, a mighty, mighty prophet." Glory to God. Thank you, Jesus for this great honor.

I am also aware that our experiences in life help prepare us for our ministry. My doctorate in education helped me to develop my writing skills. By the time Jesus told me I was going to write my first spiritual book—and He even told me the name of it, *Look What's Happening to Me. Is it Happening to You Too?*—I was not afraid because I already wrote a dissertation and co-authored a book with my daughter, *Super Parenting: Raising the Next Generation.* In my community involvement with organizations, I held local, regional, and national leadership positions and published research articles, brochures, and developed a National Teen Leadership Development Program.

One time I ran for vice president of a national organization. Oh, I prayed and campaigned hard for it, and then I lost. Instead of vice president, I was elected to be the National Program Director. At that time, I did not know that I would be authoring a National Teen Leadership Development Program that emerged to the National Teen Conference. What I did know was that I felt defeated and disappointed that I did not win the vice president position. Little did I know that Jesus was guiding and giving me the experiences I needed to help me with my ministry, teaching God's people. I looked at my not getting that position as a defeat, but Jesus put me exactly where I needed to be and experience what I needed to experience for my ministry. So here I am writing this book on the spiritual gifts of the Holy Spirit.

I am experiencing life even now in a certain way that may not look the way I want it to look. God knows best, and I know my experiences are for my own good even though for any given moment it may not appear that way. Learn the lesson in the experience. Whether you are a minister in the pulpit, ordained, or a minister among the people as one of the people, find out what you need to know to prepare and/or enhance your ministry. I am a minister among the people as one of the people, and I am still learning, enhancing, and growing in the spirit of the Lord.

The Seven Keys for Ministry

Lesson 9, "Ministry," discusses our purpose and ministry that God has for us to help His people. The seven keys that will help us understand our responsibility in serving God's people through our ministry are *ministry, people, experience, knowledge, acceptance, rejection,* and *identity.*

1. **Ministry**: Everyone has a ministry.
2. **People**: Your ministry is to help God's people.
3. **Experience**: Your experiences prepare you for your ministry.
4. **Knowledge**: Some people will know their ministry, while others will not have a clue.

5. **Acceptance**: Your need to want and accept your ministry.
6. **Rejection**: Do not run and hide or reject your ministry.
7. **Identity**: Your identity and purpose in life is in your ministry.

Key 1: Ministry

Everyone has a ministry. You are either a minister in the pulpit, ordained, or you are a minister among the people as one of the people. In life, you are preparing for your ministry as early as in your mother's womb. Your life experiences are a part of your ministry. It gets you ready. Everyone has a ministry here on Earth. Through your ministry, you are to serve God's people. Your ministry can be tied to your career or separate.

Jesus informed me of my ministries of prophecy and teacher in my morning prayers:

Your ministry is to teach my people how to perform their spiritual gifts. You will write books to teach many souls all over the world. They will read your books and learn a lot from them.

This book is the second book I have written. My first book is *Spiritual Awakening Look What's Happening to Me, Is it Happening To You Too?*

Jesus also said, *your ministry as a prophet is to help people in their problems in coping with the flesh [experiences]. You will help many save their souls.*

I do spiritual readings for Jesus. I allow people to ask questions to Jesus and Jesus will answer through me as His vessel. I help God's people deal with the earthly problems of life. I also deliver messages in my church charismatic prayer group and other messages as directed from Jesus Christ.

I am so blessed to have such a unique relationship with Jesus Christ, and I am ever so humbly grateful and honored for my anointings.

Just know everyone has spiritual gift(s) and if you do not already, pray to the Holy Spirit to have your spiritual gift(s) released to you. Pray for your ministry to be revealed to you. Your ministry will be unique to you according to your life experiences.

> As each one has received a gift, use it to serve one another as good stewards of God's varied grace. (1 Peter 4:10)

Key 2: People

Your ministry is to help serve God's people. You are to help save souls. Some of you may not know your ministry yet. Some may know but are not quite sure. Others know and would like to know more about what they are doing. Pray to the Lord and let Him lead you through the Holy Spirit. Your spiritual gifts will help you with your ministry to serve God's people. Know that your spiritual gifts from the Holy Spirit and your ministry go hand in hand. Pray for them. They will help you serve God's people.

My spiritual gifts are prophecy and teaching. My ministry in prophecy is to help people with their problems to help save their souls. My ministry in teaching is to teach God's people how to perform their spiritual gifts.

> Now in regard to spiritual gifts, brothers, I do not want you to be unaware. (1 Cor. 12:1)
>
> But everything must be done in order. (1 Cor. 14:40)

Key 3: Experience

Your life experiences help prepare you with the knowledge needed to get the job done. You will know how it feels to work with God's people because you would have "been there and done that," as they say, or have a similar experience to be able to relate.

The 3 Ministry Preparation Experiences

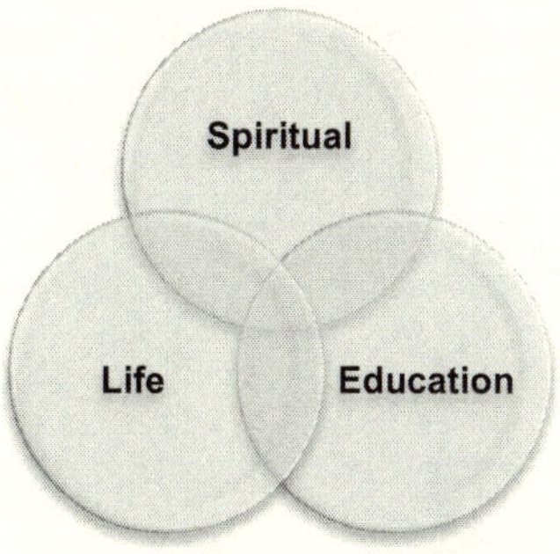

The three Ministry Preparation Experiences along with Life also includes spiritual and the education aspects. The spiritual experiences will come with such as being baptized in the spirit, attending church services, participating in church activities, supernatural events that may take place as you move toward your ministry, etc.

For example, I began to have thoughts about giving a minister a message. At first, I thought I was just thinking up stuff and it didn't really mean anything, but the thoughts kept coming back. What was so odd about it was when I started writing it down, the thoughts would stop and wait for me to write it verbatim. When I finished, the thoughts would start back up again and give more of the message. I thought to myself, *this is strange.* So, I completed the message and I ended up delivering the message to the minister. However, these thoughts went on for several weeks before I finally got around to writing the message down.

Another time I was getting my hair done at a beauty shop. As I was sitting under the dryer, thoughts started coming to me. They were sporadic messages here and there. Little did I know at that time that many more spiritual experiences were to come.

The third ministry preparation experience is education. Education can be formal or informal. "Formal" in the sense of earning degrees, certificates or attending workshops, lectures, and so on. You may informally read books such as the Bible, and other books you may read on your own that will help you toward your ministry. Note, you can also study the Bible formally as well.

The three experiences are inclusive with one another. You are getting experiences from all three and can work on them at the same time and with emphasis on one or another at any given time depending on your individual experiences needed for your ministry. I have heard people say, "Why me? Why did it happen to me?" Now you know, it is all a part of your ministry preparation.

I'd like to share an example from my life experience. For many years, I had this underlining thought that I was not quite bright enough. In my very early years, I worked in the banking industry. My name was up for a vice president position. I was so excited about it.

One morning my boss called me into the office. He started by saying, "Jacquie, you are doing a great job. You are meeting my expectations in every way." *Wow,* I thought, as he was telling me how well I was doing. Then the bombshell came down.

"Even though you are doing a good job, I do not think you are 'quite bright enough' for the position of vice president," he said.

My heart sunk. I was so disappointed. My boss did not believe in me. And I just accepted what he said and did not challenge it in any way even though I was in a very prominent position at the bank. Since then, I received a doctorate and worked through my insecurities. This happened a long time ago, but I am still able to use my experiences when I am working with God's people who are struggling with their insecurities. I have other life experience testimonies that help me with my spiritual gifts and ministry.

> . . . whereas we shall devote ourselves to prayer and to the ministry of the word. (Acts 6:4)

Key 4: Knowledge

Some of you will know in advance what you are to do in serving God, but others will not. In time, God will reveal your spiritual gift(s) and ministry to you.

Your ministry can be given to you early in life, during midlife or even later in life. When people are retiring, you may be ready for your spiritual anointing and ministry if you do not already have it.

God will help you with your ministry no matter what time in your life you may begin. The point is this: know you are driven by the Holy Spirit and His leadership. He has chosen you for a very specific ministry on this Earth. Know that you must be ready and prepared for the challenges your anointing and ministry may bring. Just know you have to keep going. Do not waver. God is in your life. You will be very pleased with it all. Prepare your ministry by ascertaining the knowledge you will need to carry out your ministry and to continue seeking knowledge during your ministry.

Know that it does not matter what time in your life when you receive your ministry. You may hear of young people and children who have an anointing on them. I started my teaching spiritual ministry later in life.

A colleague once told me about her spiritual experiences as a young girl. Her family was poor where they lived in a southern state. She remembers the days when her mother was outside in the yard and people would walk by and stop to talk to her mom.

She said, "I was five years old, and I would stand by my mom clinging to her leg. I was shy and felt safe holding my mom's leg. As my mom kept talking, I would just know things about the person. Sometimes I did not quite understand what it all meant, so I would tell my mom because I was trying to see what was going on. When my family realized I had a gift, they would stand on the corner from the grocery store with me and people would pay a nickel to hear what I had to say about them."

My colleague looked me in the eyes and said, "I had no idea what was going on until I got older. I have never used my spiritual gift in that way by asking for money. I now know that my gift is from God and that I need to use my gift the way God wants me to."

It was so fascinating to me to hear her story because I received my gifts later in life and my colleague received her gift so early in life.

This is so important. Your life is centered not around you but around your ministry. Your deeds, your behavior is of who you are, is centered around your ministry. Spiritually you are a child of God. You are to be obedient to your God. God is all good, loving, kind, joyous, and wonderful.

God is pure love. God has chosen you to read this book. This book will change your spiritual life. You will never be the same. You will come out from reading this book a holier person with perceptions you never had before reading it. Go forth and spread the Word to God's people.

> For as in one body, we have many parts, and all the parts do not have the same function, so we, though many, are one body in Christ and individually parts of one another. Since we have gifts that differ according to the grace given to us, let us exercise them: if ministry, in ministering: if one is a teacher, in teaching; . . . if one exhorts, in exhortation; if one contributes, in generosity; if one is over others, with diligence; if one does acts of mercy, with cheerfulness. (Rom. 12:4–6, 8)

Key 5: Acceptance

You must want to serve God. You will serve God through your ministry. Accept your ministry and not desire to have someone else's. God will distribute His gifts according to His own desires. Accept what God has for you.

A few years ago, I was driving a woman to an activity when the Lord told me to play the song, "The Call." I'd received the CD from a member from an organization who recorded it. So, I played the song. I knew Jesus told me to play the song for the woman who was riding with me. Wow, the song was just beautiful. When it finished, I asked her, "Is God calling you?"

She took a deep breath and said, "Yeah, He has been calling me for some time now. I just do not know if I want to do it or not."

I said to her, "When God calls, we need to be obedient to the Lord and accept." Through the grace of God, she is a pastor today and is doing well.

> But one and the same Spirit produces all of these, distributing them individually to each person as he wishes. (1 Cor. 12:11)
>
> Since we have gifts that differ according to the grace given us, let us exercise them: (Rom. 12:6)

Key 6: Rejection

Do not run and hide or reject your ministry. You are to accept your ministry. God will reward you for your obedience to performing your ministry. Who said it was going to be easy?

There was a Christian woman who was a prayer warrior in her church. She received the gift of tongues. At first, she enjoyed praying for and with church members. Then she grew tired and did not want to do it anymore. It was starting to take up a lot of her time, so she stopped. Jesus had given me the message to tell her to go back to praying for troubled members in her church. I told her that her anointing was irrevocable. I was only the messenger. She said she felt like she would go back to doing it.

I do not know what her outcome is, whether she returned to being a prayer warrior. I just delivered the message. It was up to her to determine if she was going to return to being a prayer warrior or to reject it. I often deliver messages to people that I sometimes only see once and do not know the outcome of their message.

It very well may be challenging at times. God will not give you any more than you can bear.

> Whatever you do, do it from the heart, as for the Lord and not for others, knowing that you will receive from the Lord due payment of inheritance; be slaves of the Lord Christ. (1 Colossians 3:23–24)
>
> Look to yourselves that you do not lose what we worked for but may receive a full recompense. (2 John 1:8)
>
> Therefore, do not throw away your confidence; it will have great recompense. (Hebrews 10:35)

Key 7: Identity

Your spiritual identity and purpose in life is tied to your experiences, and ministry along with your spiritual gifts. You live for the experience of your ministry. Do you get it? Your spiritual self-identity is in your purpose, your spiritual gifts, your experiences (in life, education, and spirituality), and your ministry that goes hand in hand together with your faith in God.

Spiritual Self-Identity

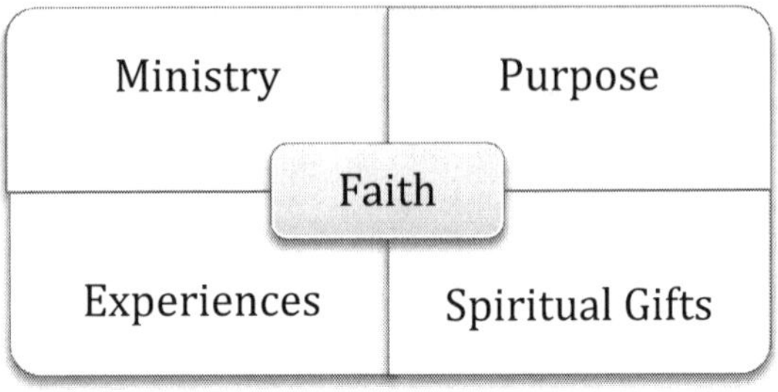

Your spiritual self-identity is in Jesus Christ. Faith, you must have faith in Jesus Christ and the Trinity (God the Father, God the Son, our Lord and Savior, and God the Holy Spirit). Your faith in God is permeated throughout your purpose, spiritual gifts, your ministry preparation experiences (life, education, and spiritual), and your ministry itself.

You are chosen, loved, and accepted by God. A part of God's spirit resides in you as He shares His Spirit with you. The Holy Spirit will distribute His spiritual gifts as He so desires that will help in your ministry to ultimately help save souls.

My spiritual self-identity is in my prophecy and teaching to God's people. This is who I truly am. I am one with the spirit connection through my spiritual gifts from the Holy Spirit doing God's work through my ministry. In my ministry of teaching, I am to teach God's people how to identify themselves, to help God's people find or develop their purpose, and spiritual gifts. In my ministry of prophecy, I am helping God's people to understand their ministry preparation experiences (life, education, and spirituality).

> We know that all things work for good for those who love God, who are called according to his purpose. (Rom. 8:28)

Summary

Lesson 9, "Ministry," is the ninth spoke in the Spiritual Wheel of GOD (the Gifts of Development). The seven keys are *ministry, people, experience, knowledge, acceptance, rejection,* and *identity.*

Everyone has a ministry. You are either a minister in the pulpit, you are ordained, or you are a minister among the people as one of the people. Your ministry is to serve God's people and to save souls. You have three categories of experience to help your ministry: life experiences, educational experiences, and spiritual experiences. You can experience them together or any combination of the three. Your experiences prepare you for your ministry, and your experiences give you the knowledge needed to get the job done. You will often know how it feels to work with God's people of your experience. Some will know their ministry, and some will not have a clue. In time, God will reveal your spiritual gift to you. You must want and accept your ministry.

You must want to serve God. You will serve God through your ministry. Accept your ministry and don't desire to have someone else's. God will distribute His gifts according to His own desires. Accept what God has for you. You must not run and hide or reject your ministry. Know that your identity is in Jesus Christ. With your faith in Jesus Christ, your spiritual self-identity is expressed through your purpose, spiritual gifts from the Holy Spirit, experiences, and ministry.

You are chosen, loved, and accepted by God, and God's spirit resides in you. God is pure love. God has chosen you to read this book. This book will change your spiritual life. You will never be the same. You will emerge a holier person with perceptions you never had before reading this book. Go forth and spread the Word to God's people.

Chapter 10
Lesson 10: Spirituality

"God is spirit, and those who worship him must worship him in spirit and truth." ~ John 4:24

Many Christians do not believe in the presence of evil spirits. It's as if evil doesn't exist until, perhaps, those non-believers indeed experience the supernatural. God believes in good, love, and kindness. Satan, the devil, believes in bad, evil, and demonic experiences. We easily accept the good, but some tend to think that evil does not exist. We must always wear the spiritual Armor of God to protect ourselves from evil.

Spiritual warfare is a mental condition. It is a determined and committed attitude of the mind. We must mentally and spiritually prepare ourselves to deal with demonic attacks.

Spirituality is the tenth and final spoke in the Spiritual Wheel of GOD (the Gifts of Development). God provides you with a mental weapon against evil with the Armor of God.

In Lesson 10, I will discuss the scriptures that were given to me by my prayer partner in the order that I received them. I also tell my testimony of when I cast out evil in three prayer members at a prayer meeting. It was the hardest assignment I have ever done to date. I also discuss another testimony of casting out evil in a colleague from school. Finally, I will discuss the seven keys of Lesson 10 that will help us understand our responsibility in serving God's people through spirituality.

Scriptures for Spirituality

The scriptures in this lesson are from the perspective of your spirituality. The scriptures speak to the spiritual gift of "preaching repentance," which is casting out demons and healing the sick. It also speaks about how to live a good spiritual life, such as the Golden Rule, the answer to your prayers, about judging others and having faith like the blind men who wanted to see. The scriptures speak to the prophet who is not without honor except in his own native place and in his own home. There are also scriptures on how to live your life to prepare you for your spiritual gifts.

> He summoned the Twelve and began to send them out two by two and gave them authority over unclean

spirits . . . He said to them, "Wherever you enter a house, stay there until you leave from there. Whatever places does not welcome you or listen to you, leave there and shake the dust off your feet in testimony against them." So, they went off and preached repentance. They drove out many demons, and they anointed with oil many who were sick and cured them. (Mark 6:7, 10–13)

Jesus said to them, "A prophet is not without honor except in his native place and among his own kin and in his own house." So, he was not able to perform any mighty deed there, apart from curing a few sick people by laying his hands on them. (Mark 6:4–5)

"Therefore, do not be afraid of them. Nothing is concealed that will not be revealed, nor secret that will not be known . . . Everyone who acknowledges me before others I will acknowledge before my heavenly Father. But whoever denies me before others, I will deny before my heavenly Father." (Matt. 10:26, 32–33)

"When they hand you over, do not worry about how you are to speak or what you are to say. You will be given at that moment what you are to say. For it will not be you who speak but the spirit of the Father speaking through you . . . Whoever receives a prophet because he as a prophet will receive a prophet's reward, and whoever receives a righteous man because he is righteous will receive a righteous man's reward." (Matt. 10: 19–20, 41)

When he entered the house, the blind men approached him and Jesus said to them, "Do you believe that I can do this:" "Yes, Lord," they said to him. Then he touched their eyes and said, "Let it be done for you according to your faith." (Matt. 9: 28–29)

Jesus turned around and saw her, and said, "Courage, daughter! Your faith has saved you." And from that hour the woman was cured. (Matt. 9:22)

Cure the sick, raise the dead, cleanse lepers, drive out demons. Without cost you have received; without cost you are to give. (Matt. 10:8)

Then he said to his disciples, "The harvest is abundant, but the laborers are few; so, ask the master of the harvest to send out laborers for his harvest. (Matt. 9:37–38)

"Ask and it will be given to you; seek and you will find; knock and the door will be opened to you. For everyone who asks, receives; and the one who seeks, finds; and to the one who knocks, the door will be opened. Which one of you would hand his son a stone when he asks for a loaf of bread, or a snake when he asks for a fish? If you then, who are wicked, know how to give good gifts to your children, how much more will your heavenly Father give good things to those who ask him. Do to others whatever you would have them do to you. This is the law and the prophets." (Matt. 7:7–12)

For as you judge, so will you be judged, and the measure with which you measure will be measured out to you. Why did you notice the splinter in your brother's eye, but do not perceive the wooden beam in your own eye? How can you say to your brother, "Let me remove that splinter from your eye," while the wooden beam is in your eye? You hypocrite remove the wooden beam from your eye first; then you will see clearly to remove the splinter from your brother's eye. Ask and it will be given to you; seek and you will find; knock and the door will be opened to you. (Matt. 7:2-7)

He turned and said to Peter, "Get behind me, Satan! You are an obstacle to me. You are thinking not as God does, but as human beings do." (Matt. 16:23)

And he was transfigured before them; his face shone like the sun and his clothes became white as light. and behold, Moses and Elijah appeared to them, conversing with him. (Matt. 17:2, 3)

. . . but Jesus came and touched them, saying, "Rise and do not be afraid." And when the disciples raised their eyes, they saw no one else but Jesus alone. (Matt. 17:7, 8)

When they came to the crowd a man approached, knelt down before him, and said, "Lord, have pity on my son, for he is a lunatic and suffers severely; often he falls into the fire, and often into the water. I brought him to your disciples, but they could not cure him." Jesus said in reply, "O faithless and perverse generation, how long will I be with you? How long will I endure you? Bring him to me." Jesus rebuked him and the demon came out of him, and from that hour the boy was cured. Then the disciples approached Jesus in private and said. "Why could we not drive it out?" (Matt. 14–19)

He said to them, "Because of your little faith. Amen, I say to you, if you have faith the size of a mustard seed, you will say to this mountain, 'move from here to there,' and it will move. Nothing will be impossible for you." (Matt. 17:20)

"Amen, I say to you, whatever you bind on earth shall be bound in heaven, and whatever you lose on earth shall be loosed in heaven. Again [Amen,] I say to you, if two of you agree on earth about anything for which they are to pray, it shall be granted to them by my heavenly Father. For where two or three are gathered in my name, there am I in the midst of them." (Matt. 18:18–20)

Jesus looked at them and said, "For human beings this is impossible, but for God all things are possible." (Matt 19:26)

"Whatever you ask for in prayer with faith, you will receive." (Matt 21:22)

Discussion of Scriptures for Spirituality

There were several scriptures in this chapter that stood out to me: Mark 6:7, 10–13, Matthew 14–19, and Matthew 16:23. I enjoyed how the Lord gave His disciples the authority over uncleaned spirits and to heal the sick. He then sent them out two by two to preach repentance. It reminds me of when the Holy Spirit gave me my spiritual gifts along with the authority to send me out to do God's will.

I also loved the story of the father with his son who suffers greatly from falls into the fire and then into the water. The father asked the Lord to have pity on him. Jesus rebuked the evil in the man's son and cured him.

From the Bible, God often demonstrated how to perform His miracles and the spiritual gifts the Holy Spirit distributes to us. Jesus led by example and continues to lead us today. I liked the way Jesus said, "Get behind me, Satan!" Gear up spiritually and get ready to go out into the world with the Armor of God and be able to say, "Get behind me, Satan!"

Which scriptures are significant to you and your personal experiences? Take a few minutes and reflect on how the scriptures relate in your life. Did a scripture stand out and resonate from within?

Lesson 10: Spirituality

In this section, I provide many excerpts from my memoirs of my communications with Jesus. This is an important lesson because it's the last one in the Spiritual Wheel of GOD. This testimony was one of the more personal experiences I've had, and it has affected me in such a deep way.

February 2, 2014
Sunday morning prayers

You will give your last lesson—Lesson 10, Spirituality—on Friday. You will speak of the spiritual battle and the Armor of God. On the last lesson, miracles will take place. Spiritual gifts will be distributed among the members. It will be a very holy day for the prayer group. People will speak about it for years to come. You will write about it, and you will go around and speak about it. You will bring some of the members who received their spiritual gifts from it with you. [At that point in time, the miracles and distribution of Spiritual gifts did not happen.]

February 3, 2014
Monday morning prayers

People are going to start coming to you. You will be very pleased with it all. You know what to do to keep going. You are well into your ministry. You are doing a great job. You are to help people with their spiritual gifts. You are to heal others. You are to cast out demons and demon influences in others. You are to give spiritual readings. You are to teach others about their spiritual awakenings through your books and lectures. You will connect loved ones with those who have crossed over. You can do it all. You can help anyone in any part of their spiritual awakening. You are the most powerful prophet on Earth during this lifetime.

February 4, 2014
Tuesday morning prayers

You will do your final lesson on Friday about spirituality. You will speak on spiritual battle. You will talk about how you must always keep your guard up to protect yourself from evil. You will talk about the evil you had to destroy in people. You will talk about the evil you exorcized out of three women in the prayer meeting. You will talk about the way you were treated that night. I will tell you what to say and to do.

This week you will tell the story of what happened. You will tell them you come from truth and how hard it was for you to be obedient to the Word. You were humiliated in front of the group. The prayer leader said that was not the way exorcisms happened.

He spoke on traditional exorcisms. In the Charismatic faith, exorcisms are done in different ways. You will also talk about the Armor of God. You will show them how you put on the Armor of God every morning. You will spend a little more time than you usually do in the prayer meeting talking about the last lesson.

February 7, 2014
Friday morning prayers

Your prayer partner will give you scriptures this morning. You will read them before you go to the prayer meeting tonight. Lesson 10, Spirituality, is the last lesson. You will talk about the spiritual warfare and the need to protect yourself with the Armor of God from Ephesians 6. You will tell them how you prepare yourself with the Armor of God in the mornings. You will talk about spiritual warfare and how you did three exorcisms in the prayer group. I will lead you through the lesson. You will do a great job.

February 7, 2014
Friday evening prayer group meeting

The prayer meeting always starts at seven p.m. with the worship songs following the greeting of one another. Right after the greeting is the sharing time. I was a little nervous this time because Jesus wanted me to share my testimony of when I did the exorcisms. As you'll see in the next section, it was a very difficult and emotional time for me. I still think about it to this day.

"Thank you all for coming," I said. "I want to share the last lesson, which is on spirituality and spiritual warfare. You must protect yourself with the Armor of God."

The group nodded and mumbled. The Armor of God is a workshop topic of its own. It was briefly mentioned at the prayer meeting.

"Jesus also wants me to share my testimony about the exorcisms of three prayer group members several years ago in 2010."

My Testimony 1: Casting Out Demons

Several attempts occurred in trying to cast out the demons in the three prayer group members. Something would come up and it would not happen. Eventually it happened on February 19, 2010.

In the beginning, I was to do an exorcism with a priest, but that did not happen. I was then instructed by Jesus to do the exorcism with the co-prayer leader, but that did not happen either. Three months later, the exorcisms did occur, but I ended up doing them by myself in the prayer group meeting with the witnesses of the prayer group members, the leader, and the co-leader.

Through excerpts, I will discuss what took place leading up to the exorcisms.

November 20, 2009
Friday morning prayers

You have other work to do. Tonight, you will be able to cast out the demons in the three people who did not come last week. They will be there tonight, and so will the priest. He is anxious to talk to you. The priest will walk over to the person who begins to act weird. You will follow him over. The priest will begin praying, and you will speak in tongues. You will tell this person when the demon is gone. Make sure that you tell them, "It is not I but the Father above. Jesus Christ cast out the demon." You and the priest will cast out the demons three times—not all at once but one after the other. Immediately after you finish the first exorcism, another person will start acting weird. You and the priest will cast out the demons until you have cast out all three. The priest knows his part in casting out the demons. He now knows you will do it with him.

The people there who will witness this will fall to their knees. They will start praying, crying in awe in what they have just witnessed. Word is going to spread among the parishes. The parish priest is going to want to talk to you right away. He will want to talk to you before others do. Remember to tell them that Jesus Christ drove out the demons, not you. I know you will obey because you are an obedient servant like no other that I have ever seen in this lifetime. That is why I have chosen you.

The priest was in awe of how you waited until he left before you went home. He knew then that you were very special and that he would be doing some work with you. Both of you have different divine paths, and you will see each other from time to time but will not work together on a regular basis. Go now, for I have spoken. Go in peace.

The exorcisms did not take place that night at the prayer meeting. So, after the prayer meeting, I went home and asked Jesus why the exorcisms didn't take place.

You did the right thing. You were obedient. For some reason, the priest was not up to working tonight. He did not do what he was supposed to do. He was somewhat depressed tonight. He didn't even want to talk to you as he wanted to before. Everyone is not as obedient as you. That is why I chose you. You are obedient and consistent in doing so. Another time will present itself for you to do the exorcisms. Don't worry. You have a lot of work ahead of you. We will talk tomorrow or this morning. Everything that you are doing is working as planned. Go now.

February 15, 2010
Monday morning prayers

Friday will be the big day. You will be casting out demons. The co-prayer leader will help you with the first one and you will do the other two alone. You have done them alone before so it will not be difficult for you. I know you will get great satisfaction out of casting out the demons.

February 17, 2010
Ash Wednesday

I saw a prayer group member on Ash Wednesday at the seven p.m. Mass service. Jesus talked to her through me. He told her to go to the next Friday prayer group meeting to get the demon cast out. He told her that she could call me anytime. When she couldn't sleep at night, she should say to evil, "I rebuke you in the name of Jesus Christ."

She said, "I want to go to church first and then I will meet you after church." The Mass was at the same time as the prayer group meeting. I told her, "I have to do what Jesus told me." She said, "I am going to call the co-prayer leader to see if I can change the time for the prayer group meeting to start after the Friday Mass." We said our goodbyes and left.

After my encounter with the prayer member, I asked Jesus how it went.

You did a good job with the prayer group member. She is the one who has legions. She will be the last of the three to cast out demons. The prayer group member knows that she has a demon in her, and she knows that it is more than one. She felt embarrassed to say it in front of you. She now understands and knows you will not judge her for having the demons. She will be there on Friday.

The co-prayer leader is going to call you to tell you that the time for the prayer meeting has changed. She is excited because she is going to witness casting out demons. Everything is going as planned. Go now. Go in peace. Jesus has spoken.

February 19, 2010
Friday morning prayers

We have lots of work to do today. You will go to the prayer meeting tonight. A prayer member has been praying very hard to have the demon removed. She has lived with demons for a very long time. She is so happy to know that they will finally be gone. She doesn't even know how to live without one.

Tonight, you will cast out the demons in her. I say "demons" because she has legions in her. She will be the third prayer group member to cast out the demons. The first prayer group member will be the person the co-prayer leader mentioned to you. The co-prayer leader will help you with her.

This prayer member will start acting strange and the co-prayer leader will walk over to her praying. You will follow her speaking in tongues. When you have removed the demon, you will say, "It is gone, it is gone." She will feel better right away. She is going to thank you. You will tell her, "It is not I but the Father above. Jesus Christ did it."

A little after that, the co-prayer leader is going to start acting strange. She will double over in pain. You will go over to her and pray tongues over her. When you are finished, you will say, "It is gone, it is gone." The co-prayer leader will thank you for being obedient to God. You will say, "It is not I but the Father above. Jesus Christ did it."

No sooner will you say that when another prayer member will start acting strange. The lights are going to blink off and on. The room will become eerie. You will walk over to her speaking in tongues. While legions are afraid of you, as all demons are because of your power through me, they will put up a fight. A fight that they will not win. Do not be afraid. You will win. When the legions are gone, the lights will go back to normal. You will say, "It is gone, it is gone." The prayer member will thank you. You will say, "It is not I but the Father above. It was Jesus Christ who did it."

Then I will speak to the group in another tone of voice. I am going to change the tone so that they know that it is Me, Jesus Christ, talking. I will talk to them to calm them down. The group is going to be amazed and shocked about what just occurred. After I talk to them, the prayer members will talk about their experience tonight. This is going to be the talk for years to come. Someone is going to run over to the directory to get the parish priest. The parish priest is going to come over to hear the experiences of the prayer group. He is going to talk to the group, and they are going to pray together thanking God for this great miracle that has occurred at the parish.

February 19, 2010
Friday evening prayer group meeting

I went to the prayer group meeting. I knew what my assignment was for that night. I was to cast out demons in three different prayer group members. As I sat in circle for worship, I was waiting for the member to start acting a little strange. I knew who it was because the co-prayer leader discussed her with me. She knew her assignment was to go over and start praying over her. I was to follow and to speak tongues to drive out the demon.

Then it happened. A member started acting strange, but it was another prayer member, someone I wasn't expecting.

The co-prayer leader did not move. I waited and the co-prayer leader still did not move. I felt relieved because I thought the exorcism would not happen because things were not going along as planned, but then Jesus spoke to me and said," you *will do all three of the exorcisms alone. The co-prayer leader decided at the last minute not to participate."*

I was scared to do it by myself. I had comfort in doing it with the co-prayer leader. But I had to be obedient to Jesus' Word, so I got up and went over to the prayer member. This prayer member had been around for some time, and she had acted strange in the prayer meetings before. She was squirming around, looking like she was very uncomfortable and in pain.

I said to her, "Do you want to get rid of it?" And she said yes. So, I proceeded to speak in exorcism tongues. They are very rough, gross, and guttural sounding. When I finished the exorcism, I told the prayer member, "It is gone, and it will never return. You can now sleep at night."

"Thank you," she said. I told her, "It is not I but the Father above. Jesus did it." She went and sat down. I was still standing there when Jesus asked me to say to the group, "There is someone in this room who has evil in them."

Another prayer group member got up. She fell face down stretched out on the floor with her arms stretched out with her body in the shape of a cross. This was the woman I had spoken to on Ash Wednesday about getting rid of the demons in her. She was supposed to be last. I asked her, "Do you want to get rid of them?" She said yes.

So, I proceeded to speak in exorcism tongues until the legions were removed. I whispered in her ear, "They are gone, and they will never return. You will be able to sleep at night." She thanked me. I told her, "It is not I but the Father above. It was Jesus Christ who did it." She went to her seat.

While standing there, Jesus told me to say, "There is someone else in this room who also needs to get rid of evil." No one moved. So, Jesus told me to say it again. "There is someone else in the room who needs to get rid of evil." No one moved. Then Jesus said to say, "I know who you are."

As soon as I said that a prayer group member got up right away and came forward. She was the one who was referred by the priest to go to the prayer meeting to get help getting rid of the evil spirit inside her. She was supposed to be the first one to have the exorcism, but she ended up being the last of the three.

I asked her the same question: "Do you want to get rid of it?" She said yes. I proceeded to speak in exorcism tongues until the evil was removed. I also whispered in her ear, "It is gone, and it will never return. You will be able to sleep at night." She thanked me and then went back to her seat.

I was still standing in front of the group. After casting out the demons, Jesus wanted to talk to the group. As Jesus was talking to the group through me, the prayer leader shouted in a deep voice, "Jacquie, sit down!" When he said the word *down*, it was like a loud boom in my head. He kept saying it.

I said to him, "I do what Jesus tells me to do. Jesus told me to be quiet, and then Jesus told me to sit down. I had to finish the prayer meeting. I wanted to go home, but I was obedient to His Word."

The prayer leader made an announcement. "I have gone to prayer meetings for over twenty years and did not see casting out of demons without scriptures."

I couldn't believe what he said. We have a charismatic prayer group that spoke of the spiritual gifts of the Holy Spirit, living in the spirit, Baptism in the Holy Spirit, and he spoke of a traditional exorcism.

At that time, I was speechless. Jesus, through me, had cast the demons out with exorcism tongues. After the prayer meeting, the prayer leader approached me privately and said, "I am sorry that I had to do that."

"I do what Jesus tells me to do," I said. The prayer leader just walked away.

Later, I read *The Charism of Tongues: A Gift of Prayer and Edification* by Fr. Michael J. Sears in which he says, "There are tongues as an instrument of exorcism," (Sears, 93).

When I returned home that night after the prayer meeting, I was devastated with what had occurred with the prayer leader. I couldn't believe he would disrespect me the way he did. Shouting at the top of his voice, "Jacquie, sit down!" He is a Charismatic prayer leader. He knows about the charismatic and spiritual gifts from the Holy Spirit. The co-prayer leader was to assist in the first exorcism. She knew what was going to happen and yet she did nothing. She didn't move. She didn't say a word. I couldn't believe this happened to me.

I started crying. I was hurt. "Dear Jesus, I did everything you told me to do. I was obedient to Your Word. How could you let this happen to me?" I cried. As I was sobbing, Jesus told me, "Even Jesus Christ was crucified." I had to stop and think about what Jesus said. It gave me a better understanding of the situation, but the pain was still there. I wanted to know why this happened to me.

So, I said to Jesus, "Dear Jesus, may I ask you a question?

Yes. Do not cry, Dr. Jacquie. You were so obedient tonight. God will reward you. I know it took a lot to hold your tongue with the prayer leader. You will be rewarded. The prayer leader will soon be your strongest supporter. He is going to experience some things that are going to make him a believer. He will need to ask you for help. You will help him, which is going to make him a believer. His wife [co-prayer leader] already knows you are strong in the Word. She is going to call to apologize for the rudeness of her husband. She is going to ask you to cast out a demon in her, but she doesn't want you to do it in the prayer meeting. You will tell her Jesus told you that she was going to call. Jesus also said that He will get rid of the demon in the prayer meeting. By allowing [you], Dr. Jacquie, to cast out the demon in the prayer meeting, she will encourage others who may have the same problem. It will be her decision. In the prayer meeting, she will need to ask to have the demon cast out of her. If she doesn't ask, so be it.

[The co-leader never asked.]

The prayer leader's attitude will change by the next prayer meeting. The three members that you cast out the demon will call him and tell him how rude he was to you. They will tell him—even though he had never seen a demon cast out that way—that it worked because it is gone.

The prayer group members will start asking you how to help them in various ways like healing, counseling, casting out demons, and helping them feel better. The parish priest is going to want to speak to you. You will wait for me to give you instructions.

You will go to the eight o'clock Mass tomorrow morning. A prayer member will approach you to apologize for the prayer leader's rudeness. You will say, "I do what Jesus tells me to do. Do you have a question for Jesus?" She will say, "Will you please heal me?" You will lay hands on her. When she says thank you, you will say "Jesus did it." You will be approached by several prayer group members. Sunday is going to be a busy time. You are going to have a lot of people coming up to you. I will tell you what to say and do.

February 20, 2010
Saturday morning prayers

I woke up the next morning crying. I was still upset. I needed to talk to Jesus.

Do not cry, Dr. Jacquie. You were obedient. You did what I told you to do. You handled the situation correctly and exactly the way I told you to do and say. The prayer leader was angry because of your power in the Word. He wants to be the leader along with his wife. He wants the group to look up to them not you. He was very rude because of his own confusion in his head. He can say anything he wants, but he cannot deny the casting out of the demons. Those three prayer members are going to give testimony of what you did. They are also going to tell the prayer leader how rude he was to you. They are going to say, "What Dr. Jacquie did, worked."

The woman we helped, who was sent by the priest, will also have a lot to say. She will say to the prayer leader, "Before the parish priest died, he told me to come to the prayer meeting because they will help you. Well, this prayer meeting did help me. Dr. Jacquie helped me. You did not have to be so rude to her. She was never rude to you. All three of us are going to give testimony of the casting out of the demons."

[The three members who were to give testimony of casting out of demons did not happen in front of the group.]

You will be rewarded for your obedience, Dr. Jacquie. The co-prayer leader knows you did what Jesus wanted you to do. She knows her husband does not understand the Word as much as you and her. She was scared to be part of it; however, she did pray while you cast out the demons. She is going to call you. She doesn't want you to stop coming. The prayer leader doesn't want you to stop coming either. A prayer member who had the demon removed has told them that she can now sleep at night and the pain is gone. She said she felt tingling, and she also felt lighter while you were casting out the demons. The prayer leaders were amazed that you did something.

The prayer leaders are going to hear about the church greeter being able to walk and no longer having pain because of you praying over her. They are going to know that you are very special. The prayer leader is going to know that what he did was wrong, and he is going to apologize to you in the prayer meeting. After he apologizes, you will say, "Jesus says you are forgiven."

[The prayer leader never apologized to me in the prayer meeting. However, the prayer leader did apologize to me privately.]

February 21, 2010
Sunday morning prayers

Several prayer meeting members are going to approach you today after Mass services. You will wait to hear what I will tell you to say and do. Do not worry, you will never be embarrassed again. When you do God's work, you will be rewarded for it. Everyone knew that you were powerful in the Word before you started casting out the demons, and now they know you are even more powerful than they thought. The prayer leader only fooled himself. He has already found that out. All three members who we cast out the demons have called the co-prayer leader and told her that it worked. They no longer have demons inside of them.

So, perk up for church. We still have work to do. The prayer group member going through chemotherapy is going to approach you today. She has heard what happened in the prayer meeting. She is going to ask you to help her. She is going to say, "I have prayed to Jesus." You will say, "Jesus told me you would approach me today after hearing what happen in prayer meeting."

You will ask her, "What do you want Jesus to do? She will say to heal her cancer. You will then lay hands on her. Right away she is going to feel better. She is going to thank you. You will say, "It is not I but the Father above. Jesus Christ did it." She will thank you for being obedient to God.

You are coming along just fine now. You are doing a good job. Don't be gun-shy. You cannot be touched by anyone. You are gaining a popular reputation. People like and look up to you. Now it is the prayer leader who is embarrassed for what he said in the prayer meeting. The co-prayer leader is going to say to him, "I told you she was very powerful in the Word and that you should not have done what you did." The co-prayer leader also feels ashamed. Unlike the prayer leader, you will make them feel better among the prayer group.

February 22, 2010
Monday morning prayers

The word is out about you. The prayer leader realizes that he was rude and wrong for stopping you. The prayer leader and the co-prayer leader know they need to call you to see if you are still coming to the prayer meeting on Friday. Don't worry, they will never embarrass you again. No one will ever embarrass you. I will protect you.

The experience with the exorcisms with the prayer members was a true test for me from God. I had to have faith and the courage to do what Jesus wanted me to do and at the time when He wanted it done. What touched me the most was when I was being selfish about my feelings of pain and humiliation in the prayer meeting and Jesus had to pull me back into the present moment and say, "Even I was crucified." It made my pain and humiliation minuscule to Jesus' crucifixion. It was soothing to know that Jesus would not allow me to be humiliated again and that He will protect me.

My Testimony 2: The Deliverance of Evil

Prior to my morning class lecture as a college educator, I assisted a colleague in deliverance of evil in her office. She was having problems sleeping with aches and pains. The doctors could not find anything wrong with her physically. She knew she was dealing with evil and wanted to get rid of it. When Jesus told me about my colleague and her deliverance, it did not happen right away.

Jesus first told me on November 19, 2009, that I would go to school with the expectation of helping my colleague, but nothing happened. That is another way I learned about the timing of things and spiritual events taking place. Sometimes it would happen right away, and sometimes it could be a week, month, or several months or so on. In this case, it was several weeks. It finally happened on December 2, 2009.

I will discuss the deliverance through my memoirs in chronological order.

November 10, 2009
Thursday morning prayers

I am so lucky that the message of Jesus has become firmly planted in me that I lack no spiritual gift that I need. (1 Corinthians 2:11–14.)

"Good morning, Jesus. Do you have anything to say?"

Yes. You are coming along just fine. You have more work to do. You will see the person who didn't come up to you at school who needed to have a demon removed. She is extremely uncomfortable and will ask for your help. She is aware of your gifts through someone else. She will approach you this morning. She will ask you to come into her office to talk for a few minutes. You will go. As soon as she asks you to go to her office, you will know that she is the one. You will speak in tongues and remove the demon from her. When it leaves, you will say, "It is gone." Remember, you must tell her, "It is not I but the Father above. Jesus Christ removed the demon." Go in peace. I have spoken.

I went to school, but it did not happen. So, I asked Jesus why my colleague didn't ask me to help her remove the demon.

Today was not the day. She did not choose to ask you for some reason. She may be hesitant, but she will get around to asking you. She called you into her office, but she got cold feet. She played it off with the e-mail problem. As soon as she called you into the office, you knew it was her, and you were right. She will ask you soon.

December 1, 2009
Tuesday morning prayers

Today you will drive out the demon in your colleague at school. She is ready. This demon is giving her a lot of irritation. She wants to ask you, but she is uncomfortable in asking. She will approach you and tell you how she feels. When she starts talking about it, tell her that Jesus told you to drive a demon out of her. Ask her if that is okay with her. If she says yes, then you will speak tongues until you drive the demon out. You will then say, "It is gone. It is gone." She will feel a difference right away. Remember to say, "It is not I but the Father above. Jesus Christ drove out the demon." She will be so grateful for your obedience to Me. Go now. Go in peace.

For some reason, my courage was a little shaky. I wanted to make sure that it was Jesus talking to me. After all, this was now outside of the church setting and in my job location. So, I asked Jesus if it was Him speaking to me. As usual, He knew my question before I could even ask it.

Yes. You know that I am talking to you. You will drive the demon out of your colleague this morning. Go. I have spoken.

When I got to work that morning, I was on the lookout for my colleague. Then I saw her in the hallway at school. We spoke and we began talking, so I followed her into her office.

She told me that she was having problems and the doctor couldn't find anything medically wrong with her. Jesus had already told me that I would cast a demon out of her—He had been saying that for a few weeks, and now it looked like today was the day for it to happen.

The moment came for me to ask her the question. "Jesus told me that I was to drive a demon out of you. Do you want to get rid of it?" I asked. And she said yes. I asked her if I could pray over her and she said yes.

She sat up straight, placed her hands together in her lap, and closed her eyes as she waited for me to lay hands on her and pray in tongues to get rid of the demon.

The tongues were rough, harsh, and guttural sounding. When I finished, I said, "It is gone, and it will never return. You can now sleep at night." She thanked me for helping her. She said she had felt a tingling sensation when I was praying over her and then it was gone.

I told her, "It is not I but the Father above. Jesus Christ did all the work." She hugged me and whispered in my ear, "Thank you so much for being obedient to the Lord." I told her she was welcome.

I thanked Jesus for allowing me to be His vessel. I asked Him why it took so long for me to have the chance to cast out evil in my colleague.

You were obedient. Sometimes plans will change at the last minute. You did a great job. Your colleague will finally sleep all night for the first time in a long time. She will always remember what you have allowed Me to do for her. Get some rest tonight because you will be back working again. Go now. Go in peace. I have spoken.

You see how it works? God determines our assignments and the timing of them. That is why it is so important that we can communicate with the Holy Spirit and those who are prophets with Jesus Christ Himself. It is work, and we must listen so we can be obedient to God's Word. We all have a ministry, and we must keep ourselves safe through protecting ourselves with the Armor of God. We, too, can be attacked by the evil one.

The Seven Keys for Spirituality

Lesson 10 discusses our spirituality with the Armor of God to protect ourselves from evil. We must mentally and spiritually prepare ourselves to deal with demonic attacks. The seven keys will help us understand our responsibility in serving God's people and understanding our spirituality of good versus evil.

These seven keys for spirituality are *awareness*, the *Armor of God, the Helmet of Salvation and the Breastplate of Righteousness, the Belt of Truth, the Shield of Faith, the Sword of the Word and the Shoes of the Gospel of Peace,* and *deliverance.*

1. **Awareness**: Always keep your guard up to protect yourself from evil.
2. **Armor of God**: Protect yourself spiritually with the Armor of God.
3. **The Helmet of Salvation** and the **Breastplate of Righteousness**
4. **The Belt of Truth**
5. **The Shield of Faith**
6. **The Sword of the Word** and the **Shoes of the Gospel of Peace**
7. **Deliverance:** Deliverance of evil. One must distinguish between confrontational and non-confrontational deliverance.

Key 1: Awareness

There is a spiritual battle going on in this world. It is good versus evil, God versus Satan. You need to be ready for the battle. Evil sneaks around, lurking in the darkness, waiting to pounce on you. You must always be ready. You alone cannot fight Satan, the evil one. It is God who fights the battle through you. It is Jesus Christ who does all the work. You fight the battle in the name of Jesus Christ who gives you the authority to do so.

In 2012, I was lecturing in class and I noticed one of my students appeared fidgety, agitated, and could not keep himself focused on the lectures. One day in my morning prayer, Jesus told me that I was going to cast out a demon from someone in my class. So, I prepared myself for class. I read the Bible and prayed that I would be able to complete my assignment for the Lord.

I was not quite sure which student it would be because Jesus did not tell me. I lectured in class that morning when I saw the same student again becoming agitated and unable to focus on the lecture. I waited until class was over and I approached him. I asked him, "How are you doing today. Is everything okay?" He said in a quiet, low voice, "I'm okay." I told him, "Jesus told me, He is answering your prayer today." The student looked surprised and said, "He is?" I asked him, "Do you want to get rid of it?" He said, "yes."

By this time students were leaving my class and other students were coming in for the next scheduled class. The classroom was on the second floor so I asked him, "Would you like to go down to the stairwell?" He agreed. So, we went there. I asked him again, "Do you want to get rid of it?"

He said, "Yes. I played some games with my buddies and I have been this way ever since."

I asked him, "May I pray over you?" He said yes. I spoke the exorcism tongues over him until the evil left his body. I then whispered in his ear, "Your prayer has been answered. It is gone. It is gone. It will not return, and you will be able to now sleep at night." The student said, Thank you, Professor." I told him, "It is not I but the Father above. It was Jesus Christ who did it." He thanked me for being obedient to the Lord.

I really felt good helping this student. He was barely passing in class. After the exorcism, he was able to focus, complete his assignments, and he passed the class.

Awareness is very important with the Armor of God. You must use your instruments of the Bible and the spoken Word from Jesus Christ to battle evil.

> Spiritual warfare is real.
>
> For our struggle is not with flesh and blood but with the principalities, with the powers, with the world rulers of this present darkness, with the evil spirits in the heavens. Therefore, put on the Armor of God that you may be able to resist on the evil day and, having done everything, to hold your ground. (Eph. 6:12–13)
>
> So, submit yourselves to God. Resist the devil, and he will flee from you. (James 4:7)

Key 2: Armor of God

God gives us the spiritual Armor of God, the spiritual weapon to prepare us for the spiritual warfare, to help you to be ready at all times. The Armor of God helps to protect yourself from evil. The spiritual warfare is mainly the matter of the mind. The Armor of God helps to protect yourself from evil. You cannot utilize the Armor of God without a relationship with Jesus Christ. We have the authority of Jesus Christ against the devil.

Both Satan and God are supernatural. They have powers humans do not have. It is through Jesus Christ and the Holy Spirit that we are able to utilize the Armor of God. You can fight the evil in the name of Jesus Christ who gives you the authority to use His powers.

> Finally, draw your strength from the Lord and from his mighty power. Put on the Armor of God so that you may be able to stand firm against the tactics of the devil. For our struggle is not with flesh and blood but with principalities, with power, with the world rulers of this present darkness, with the evil spirits in the heavens. Therefore, put on the Armor of God that you may resist on the evil day and, having done everything, to hold your ground. So, stand fast with your loins girded with truth, clothed with righteousness as a breastplate, and your feet shod in readiness for the gospel of peace. In all circumstances, hold faith as a shield, to quench all [the] flaming arrows of the evil one. And take the helmet of salvation and the sword of the spirit, which is the word of God. (Eph. 6:10–17)

Key 3: The Helmet of Salvation and the Breastplate of Righteousness

The Armor of God has the metaphor of the Roman soldiers' weaponry from the first and second centuries. The Armor of God uses the soldiers' primary weaponry: the helmet, breastplate, loin belt, shield, sword, and shoes.

The Helmet of Salvation covers the mind tightly not allowing the devil to take you captive. The Helmet helps protects your mind from evil if you read the scriptures. The scriptures renew your mind that becomes your spiritual helmet. The devil plays mind games, is deceitful, and will attack you. You need to monitor your thoughts.

For example, I remember a true story I read years ago, and it stuck in my head ever since. A woman was sitting close to the back of the bus. A man was sitting in the back of the bus with his young children ages between three and seven. The children were jumping up and down. They were acting wild and making a lot of noise. The woman thought it was just terrible for the kids to be so out of control, so she continued her self-negative thoughts. She went on and on in her mind to say, "this is just a disgrace. Does he not hear his children? He should make them sit down and be quiet on the bus."

She continued negative fuss talking to herself until finally she could not take any more. She got up and confronted the dad about his children.

She walked up to him and with a big sigh to try to calm herself down, she said, "excuse me." The dad seemed to be preoccupied staring straight ahead. So, the woman said again, "excuse me." The man finally looked up at her. The woman said, "your children are making a lot of noise back here and they are disturbing the rest of us on the bus. Could you please quiet them down and make them sit in their seats?"

The man said, "They were just told that their mother went to Heaven and they will not see her anymore." He then stared straight ahead.

The woman was shocked. "Oh, I am so sorry, condolences to you and your children," she said. He just nodded as she went back to her seat.

This woman allowed the devil to play games with her mind, putting all kinds of negative thoughts in it. How often had you thought of someone doing negative things to you only to find out it was just something you made up in your mind? It sounded logical, right? Your logical mind with evil can work against your spiritual mind if you do not allow the Holy Spirit to work with you. You need to surrender to God. Be at peace with yourself.

When wearing the Breastplate of Righteousness that covers the heart, you must have the right frame of mind to deal with the devil. If you are mentally and emotionally defeated before you go into battle with the devil, you will be defeated. The Breastplate of Righteousness helps you to develop righteousness in your life and learn how to view yourself through Jesus Christ and the cross. You must know you are righteous in Jesus Christ and have faith in Him.

For example, I recall the time when I was in junior high school in the eighth grade. We were in the schoolyard for recess. We used to play a game where you hit the volleyball and run to the bases like in baseball. On that day, when the bell rung to go back to class, I accidently hit a student in the head with the ball. The student was a bully and was known for always beating up on students after school.

When I hit her in the head, I put my hand over my mouth and said, "Oh my God. What have I have done?"

The students laughed when she was hit with the ball. The other students pointed to me. The bully shouted at me, "Hey, come over here!" She kept waving me over, calling me all sorts of cuss words. My friend said, "You better go, or she will be picking on you for the rest of the year."

As I walked over, I started praying. I knew I could not look scared. So, I prayed to Jesus to give me strength. I felt better after praying. I stood tall and I went over and said, "I am sorry for hitting you with the ball. It was an accident."

"No, it wasn't," she snapped. "You did it on purpose. Meet me after school down the street."

Jesus had me pumped up. I said "okay" with conviction. As I walked away, my insides started trembling. I prayed again for Jesus to give me courage. My friend was nice enough to go with me to meet the bully after school. Well, through the grace of God she never showed up, and I did not have any problems with her after that.

What I did not realize at that time was that Jesus helped me with the Breastplate of the spiritual Armor of God. Jesus gave me the courage to stand tall in the name of Jesus Christ. I could have been defeated going over to her all scared and afraid of her. I did not know it then, but Jesus fights our battles against evil. She was evil going around picking on students and beating them up. We must be anchored in the grace of Jesus Christ, the Breastplate of Righteousness in the spiritual Armor of God.

> But since we are of the day, let us be sober, putting on the breastplate of faith and love and the helmet that is hope for salvation. (1 Thess. 5:8)
>
> And take the helmet of salvation and the sword of the spirit, which is the word of God. (Eph. 6:17)

Key 4: The Belt of Truth

The Belt of Truth is the only spiritual weapon that is in a physical form, the Bible. God's written words (logos) are powerful and a force to be reckoned with. Read the Bible.

For example, the loin belt for the Roman's weaponry seems insignificant. It is just a belt, right? However, when a soldier takes the belt off, his pants might fall down, his shirt becomes untucked, and he could look disarray. It is easy to fall apart without your belt on that holds everything together. The belt represents the Bible. The Bible is the written word that spiritually holds everything together. If you ignore the Word of God through the Bible in your life living it on a daily basis, your entire spiritual life can fall apart. You read and live the Bible. It is the Bible that tells us how to live. You will know not to allow the devil to trick you because you know the Bible will tell you how to live.

> So, stand fast with your loins girded in truth . . . (Eph. 6:14)

> Be eager to present yourself as acceptable to God, a workman who causes no disgrace, imparting the word of truth without deviation. (2 Tim. 2:15)

Key 5: The Shield of Faith

When you have strong faith in God, you will have a strong shield against the devil. The Shield of Faith goes hand and hand with the Belt of Truth, the Bible.

In the Roman's weaponry, the shield is attached to the belt of the soldiers and is inseparable. It is an example of your Shield of Faith is attached to the Belt of Truth that is also inseparable in the spiritual Armor of God. Your faith is attached to the Word of God. If you do not have the Word of God—the Bible in your life—it will be difficult to strengthen your faith. The Shield of Faith and the Belt of Truth, the Bible, go hand in hand.

> In all circumstances, hold faith as a shield, to quench all [the] flaming arrows of the evil one. (Eph. 6:16)
>
> . . . who by the power of God are safeguarded through faith . . . (1 Peter 1:5)

Key 6: The Sword of the Word and the Shoes of the Gospel of Peace

Discussion will take place with the Sword of the Word of God and the Shoes of the Gospel of Peace. The battles with the devil may not be every day. In the world, people fight but may not constantly fight every day. Nations may battle, or even have wars, but not every day. It is more like periods at a time. It is the same way with the spiritual battle. It may not be every day, but when evil comes, you will need to be equipped with the spiritual weaponry like the Roman soldiers.

The Romans' weaponry for the sword was a weapon to murder and kill their opponents. The most aggressive spiritual weapon God has given you is the Sword of the Word of God that has the potential to abolish evil.

Rhema is the spoken word from God. It is when the Holy Spirit speaks to us supernaturally. The sword is the symbol of the spoken word from Holy Spirit. There are times when we need to hear from the Holy Spirit to help us and guide us. The Holy Spirit may give a word in your hearts that may remind you of a scripture or even give direction as to what you are to do.

As an example, Jesus gives me the words for exorcism. If someone is acting strange, He prepares me by giving me the words to say. And when I begin the exorcism, the tongues I speak comes from Jesus. Jesus proceeds and rips the evil out of the person.

Another example is when I had trouble getting rid of the evil spirit of anger inside of me. I had done my Spiritual Freedom Check meditation one morning and one of the spirits I wanted to get rid of was the evil spirit of anger.

After the meditation, I felt better. Later that morning, I was speaking to someone who brought up the spirit of anger again. I blurted out as I bent over from a sitting position, "I am so -o-o angry." As I was speaking, my mouth opened as if I were going to vomit but nothing came out. I continued talking, and in-between the spiritual vomit, I would say, "Yes, Jesus, get rid of it." And the spiritual vomit kept coming out until it was all gone. It was a feeling of relief the same way you would feel after a big vomit took place. I just sat there for a few minutes grasping for air and feeling relieve that it was all over. "Huh," I said to myself, "what happened?" I do know I felt better afterwards and the anger in me was gone. The Sword of the Word of God is so powerful.

The shoes are the Gospel of Peace. The Romans' weaponry for shoes were not ordinary shoes. They were usually made out of brass and the bottom of the shoes were spikes.

In the spiritual Armor of God, the Shoes of the Gospel of Peace are a spiritual weaponry used against evil and to keep out negative spirits. Peace is a weapon against evil. You need to have peace with God and also with your lives, minds, and emotions. With a good foundation of peace, we can stand strong in our faith against evil spirits such as worry, depression, stress, and any other evil.

> And take the helmet of salvation and the Sword of the Spirit, which is the Word of God. (Eph. 6:17)
>
> Indeed, the word of God is living and effective, sharper than any two-edged sword, penetrating even between soul and spirit, joints, and marrow, and able to discern reflections and thoughts of the heart. No creature is concealed from him, but everything is naked and exposed to the eyes of him to whom we must render an account. (Hebrews 4:12–13)
>
> . . . and your feet shod in readiness for the gospel of peace. (Eph. 6:15)

> And let the peace of Christ control your hearts . . . (Col. 3:15)
>
> For, although we are in the flesh, we do not battle according to the flesh, for the weapons of our battle are not of flesh but enormously powerful, capable of destroying fortresses. We destroy arguments and every pretension raising itself against the knowledge of God and take every thought captive in obedience to Christ. (2 Cor. 10:3–5)

Key 7: Deliverance

Deliverance sets your soul free. Delivering and releasing you from the strong hold of the evil one, the devil, Satan himself.

Confrontational Deliverance is when a person is unable to get rid of the evil themselves. Someone must assist you (i.e., priests, clergymen, ministers, etc.) and confront the evil head on directly by calling it by its name and commanding it to leave through performing an exorcism.

Non-confrontational Deliverance is when the person can rid themselves of the evil spirits. Examples of those kinds of evil spirts are shame, fear, anger, rejection, depression, confusion, control, worry, doubt, jealousy, etc. Jesus has provided you with the Spiritual Freedom Check Meditation to assist you with these types of evil spirits (see Lesson 1, "Preparation," key 1).

> Now the Lord is the Spirit, and where the Spirit of the Lord is, there is freedom. (2 Cor. 3:17)
>
> Be free, without using freedom as a pretext for evil, but as slaves to God. (2 Peter 2:16)
>
> O Lord, my rock, my fortress, my deliverer . . . (Sam. 22:2.)
>
> Be pleased, O Lord, to deliver me; O Lord, make haste to help me. (Psalm 40:13, NKJV)
>
> So, submit yourselves to God. Resist the devil, and he will flee from you. (James 4:7)
>
> . . . . and you will know the truth and the truth will set you free. (John 8:32)

Summary

Lesson 10, "Spirituality," is the tenth and last spoke in the Spiritual Wheel of GOD (the Gifts of Development). Lesson 10 discusses spirituality from the perspective of spiritual warfare. The seven keys are *awareness, the Armor of God, the Helmet of Salvation and the Breastplate of Righteousness, the Belt of Truth, the Shield of Faith, the Sword of the Word and the Shoes of the Gospel of Peace,* and *deliverance.*

In the spiritual battle of good versus evil, you must always keep your guard up to protect yourself from evil. You alone cannot fight Satan, the evil one. It is God who fights the battle through you.

God gives you the Armor of God, the spiritual weapon to prepare you for the spiritual battle. Be ready at all times. You need to protect yourself with the Armor of God, the Helmet of Salvation, the Breastplate of Righteousness, the Belt of Truth, the Shield of Faith, the Sword of the Word, and the Shoes of the Gospel of Peace.

In the Armor of God is the Helmet of Salvation and the Breastplate of Righteousness. The Helmet of Salvation protects the mind and doesn't allow the devil to take you captive.

In the Breastplate of Righteousness, you must have the right frame of mind to deal with the devil. If you are mentally and emotionally defeated before you go into battle with the devil, you will be defeated. The Breastplate of Righteousness helps you to develop righteousness in your life and learn how to view yourself through Jesus and the cross. You must know you are righteous in Christ (Ephesians 6:10–18).

The Belt of Truth is the only spiritual weapon that is in a physical form, the Bible. God's written words (*logos*) are powerful and a force to be reckoned with.

The Shield of Faith is having strong faith in God. You have a strong shield against the evil one (Ephesian 6:16).

The Sword of the Word is *Rhema*, the spoken word from God (Ephesians 6:17.) It is when the Holy Spirit speaks to us supernaturally. God has also given the Shoes of Peace as a Weapon of Peace—the peace with Christ and the peace of Christ (Ephesians 6:15).

Besides the Armor of God, one must know of and understand the deliverance of evil. *Deliverance* is liberation for your soul. It removes the evil spirits in and/or around you, allowing you to be set free from bondage.

Confrontational deliverance is when you confront the devil head on by calling it by its name, and it's usually when the person is unable to get rid of the evil themselves. They will need assistance (exorcism). Non-Confrontational Deliverance is when the person can rid themselves of the evil spirits by calling the evil spirits by its name and rebuking it in the name of Jesus Christ. In this book, Jesus has given you the Spiritual Freedom

Check Meditation (See Lesson 1 Preparation, Key 1) that can also assist you.

To stay free, you must make changes in your life. Recognize evil, call it by its name, and rebuke in the name of Jesus Christ and/or perform Spiritual Freedom Check Meditations.

> He turned and said to Peter, "Get behind me, Satan! You are an obstacle to me. You are thinking not as God does, but as human beings do." (Matt. 16:23)

Chapter 11
Summary

". . . for nothing will be impossible for God." ~ Luke 1:37

This book is about the awareness and development of your spiritual gifts from the Holy Spirit. Your ministry is a lifetime commitment of work and obedience through using your spiritual gift(s).

> There are different kinds of spiritual gifts but the same spirit; . . . to each individual the manifestation of the Spirit is given for some benefit. To one is given through the expression of wisdom; to another the expression of knowledge according to the same Spirit; to another faith by the same Spirit; to another the gifts of healing by the one spirit; to another mighty deeds; to another prophecy; to another discernment of spirits; to another variety of tongues; to another interpretation of tongues. But one and the same Spirit produces all of these, distributing them individually to each person as he wishes. (1 Cor. 12:4, 7–11)

By reading this book, it has prepared you and allowed you to understand and implement your spiritual gifts. After reading this book, I hope it has given you a better understanding of what is expected of you when you receive as well as maintain your spiritual gifts and helps you to have a better relationship with the Holy Spirit.

Jesus introduced the Spiritual Wheel of GOD (the Gifts of Development).

Jesus told me:

You will develop the Spiritual Gifts of Development Wheel [the Spiritual Wheel of GOD]. The spokes will branch out to ten different lessons, and in the middle of the wheel will be God who is sending and receiving messages and giving directions on how to develop and perform your gift(s).

The Spiritual Gifts of Development [the Spiritual Wheel of GOD] moves among His people. It is constantly moving because things are constantly changing. It is a moving, living wheel. To perform your gifts well, you must understand the 10 lessons [spokes] within the Spiritual Gifts of Development [the Spiritual Wheel of GOD].

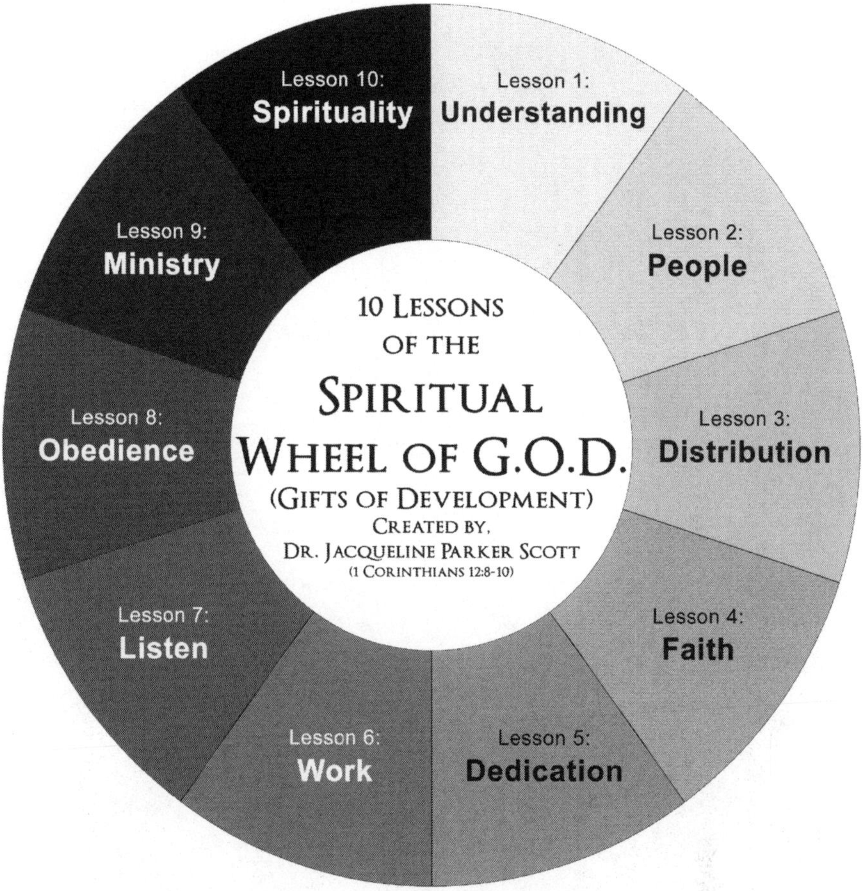

In your quest for spiritual awakening, you must understand how the spiritual gifts works. Not only do you have to understand how they work, but you must also know how to implement them. You will need to know when and how. Timing is everything. The Lord, Jesus Christ, revealed ten lessons to me in the Spiritual Gifts of Development (the Spiritual Wheel of GOD). Jesus gave me the lessons (spokes) in this particular order, which is the way that people should understand how to experience spiritual awakening of the spiritual gifts. The scriptures I received set the tone for the lessons. I would recommend documenting the scriptures in each lesson that really resonate with you and pray over what they mean to you. How do the scriptures fit into your purpose and ministry? Let the Holy Spirit lead you.

True testimonies were given for each lesson that provided examples to demonstrate the meaning of the lesson. Do you have a testimony, or do you know of someone who does? How can you equate your life to the lessons?

Jesus provided seven keys for each lesson. The keys are the elements and process for each lesson. They define the playing field, the rules.

Jesus began with the first five lessons (spokes) of the Spiritual Wheel of GOD. These five lessons introduce and explain the spiritual gifts: *preparation, people, distribution, faith,* and *dedication.*

Once you receive your gifts the remaining five lessons (spokes) show you how to perform and implement them: *work, listen, obedience, ministry*, and *spirituality.*

Here is a quick recap of each lesson on the Spiritual Wheel of GOD:

Lesson 1 is *preparation.* You need to prepare yourself to receive your spiritual gift. When you first begin to experience supernatural events, you need to be prepared, as something spiritual may begin to happen to you. Jesus introduced you to the Spiritual Freedom Check meditation to assist in removing evil spirits. The testimony was of evil snatching my spirit out of my body.

Lesson 2 is *people.* It is important to know that the spiritual gift is for God's people and not for you. You are introduced to the Listening Prayer. You will receive your blessings through someone else's spiritual gifts. I learned this lesson through my testimony when I locked my keys in the trunk of my car.

Lesson 3 is *distribution.* God distributes His spiritual gifts according to His will. Accept the gifts given to you and the responsibility that goes along with them. The testimony was on healing a colleague's leg.

Lesson 4 is *faith.* To receive your spiritual gift(s) you must have faith. You must believe you can do it through the Holy Spirit. My testimony was having enough faith to deliver a message to someone who didn't expect it, and to do as Jesus commanded me to do with the church greeter in healing her to walk without her cane.

Lesson 5 is *dedication.* It takes dedication and devotion to God to perform your spiritual gifts to God's people. The testimony was when I went to the morning church service on my day off to meet someone who never showed up and I was not able to deliver the message.

The second part of the book was the remaining five spokes of the Spiritual Wheel of GOD on implementing the spiritual gifts: *work*, *listen*, *obedience*, *ministry*, and *spirituality.*

Lesson 6 is *work.* The spiritual gift(s) alone is not enough; you must work to help save souls. The testimony was how I, as a vessel of God, healed a man's hand who did not know God was going to heal it.

Lesson 7 is *listen*. Hear the Holy Spirit so you will know what to do. Listen to the Holy Spirit through daily prayer, the Listening Prayer. You may be given assignments. The testimony was of me listening to God and my casual talks with God in understanding paranormal groups.

Lesson 8 is *obedience*. Obey the Holy Spirit and perform the assignments given to you. God will not lead you astray. The testimony was from a prayer member regarding a young boy who was dying of cancer. I gave a testimony on how I knew I had to be obedient to Jesus at a national convention and wait for someone to come to me for His message even though she wasn't expecting one.

Lesson 9 is *ministry*. I am a minister among the people as one of the people. Everyone has a ministry as either an ordained minister or a minister among the people as one of the people. In the *ministry preparation experiences,* there are three areas of knowledgeable experiences that you will need for your ministry: life, education, and spiritual experiences. Your *spiritual self-identity* begins with faith, having faith in God is first and foremost: God the father, God the Son, our Lord and Savior, and God the Holy Spirit. Your faith in God permeates throughout your purpose, spiritual gifts, your *ministry preparation experiences*, and your ministry itself.

If you do not already know your ministry, pray to the Holy Spirit to receive it. The testimony was on my ministry when Jesus told me I was a minister among the people as one of the people. My ministry is a prophet who helps people save their spirituality souls and a teacher who teaches people about their spiritual gifts.

Lesson 10 is *spirituality*. In spiritual warfare, you must protect yourself from evil spirits. God provided us with an instrument of protection from evil with the spiritual Armor of God. The testimony was on casting out of evil in the prayer meeting. I also discussed another testimony of casting out evil in a colleague.

These ten lessons are about your relationship with the Holy Spirit and the charismatic spiritual gifts. For most it will be about the Holy Spirit. I have had the honor of being able to speak with Jesus Christ directly. In my quest and thirst to have a special relationship with Jesus, I took a seminar at my parish. I am baptized in the Spirit through my special relationship with Jesus. Each day of the Life in the Spirit Seminar brought me closer and closer to Jesus. God will use you as much as you allow Him to through your obedience to Him.

To receive your spiritual gifts—if you have not already—you must first want them. Then you will need to pray to the Holy Spirit and establish a relationship. Ask the Holy Spirit to reveal your spiritual gifts. Ask the Holy Spirit to guide you in your purpose and ministry. Allow your life to be guided by the Holy Spirit. Understand that the spiritual gifts are irrevocable. Once you receive them, there is no turning back.

Just like we have a mental weapon of protection against evil with the Armor of God, we also have a mental tool to use in a metaphor of the Spiritual Wheel of GOD (the spiritual Gifts of Development) in understanding and implementing the spiritual gifts. The spiritual gifts are used to serve God's people.

Jesus also gave us the Spiritual Freedom Check Meditation to fight the spiritual demons that try to creep up in our daily lives.

Jesus said:

Freedom Check meditations are the way to have good maintenance to keep the negative triggers from past experiences away and to practice keeping the soul swept out and cleansed of negative thought debris. It is when you allow negative thought to build up when things begin to get out of hand.

When you are with a negative evil spirit, you do negative evil things. When you are in a loving and kind spirit, you will do loving and kind things.

I know my life as a prophet is constantly changing. I am learning and understanding My Lord, Jesus Christ, more and more each day.

Each day can bring something different into our lives to help us go out and serve God's people. There may be challenges, but God doesn't give us anything we cannot bear.

Lean on the Holy Spirit for guidance. The Holy Spirit is that sixth sense you have when you feel in your gut to do something one way or another. Do we listen to it, or do we just do what we want anyway and later say, "Wow, I should have followed my first thought, my gut feeling."

It is time, if you have not already, to develop that sixth sense with the Holy Spirit. This book has provided you with the tools to do so. It is up to you when you receive the spiritual gift(s) to know what to do with it and how to continue to nurture and serve God's people.

When you leave this earth, you should want to be able to say:

> Yet I consider life of no importance to me, if only I may finish my course and the ministry that I received from the Lord God, to bear witness to the gospel of God's grace. (Acts 20:24)

Amen.

Appendix 1

This is a true testimony from a charismatic prayer group member on how she received her spiritual gift of prophecy.

Please note: This testimony was written by a charismatic prayer group member, so the first person-narrator "*I*" reflects her view.

The Spiritual Gift of Prophecy

I have the gift of prophecy. I cannot really pinpoint when I received the gift, but I would say maybe within the last five years (2011). At the beginning, I thought that maybe the messages I had been receiving was just from my own mind and not from God, but later I realized it was from Him. I hear the Holy Spirit by getting messages in my mind. Sometimes, I hear somebody talking to me directly, but sometimes I just get a thought that is so strong that I can't help but pay attention it.

I was able to give a message using the spiritual gift of prophecy at a prayer meeting. It was about four years ago (2012), and the co-prayer group leader said something like, "Someone who has the gift of prophecy do not be afraid to speak out." With encouragement I was able to come out and proclaim it.

When I was at prayer meetings in the beginning, I would get a message, but I did not want to speak it out to the group. I would ask myself if the message just came from me or from the Lord. I didn't want to give fake messages so I would normally just stay quiet even when I did receive the messages. Then a time came that I could not be quiet anymore. I learned from our prayer meeting that the message is not only for me. That I should not be selfish to hold on to the message since it may be for somebody else. For instance, maybe God wanted to motivate someone who needs motivation. Or maybe someone is in confusion and needs guidance and comfort.

Sometimes I will receive a message for a specific person. But at the beginning, as usual, I thought it was just me who wanted to talk to the person about this idea. But then later I realized that God gave it to me to deliver to that specific person. Sometimes, I also receive messages for myself to be followed by a series of confirmations in different ways. Sometimes I will hear the confirmation from a very pious person, or sometimes I will read it from the Bible or from a religious article, or sometimes I will hear from a song, or sometimes I will dream about it. The dreams would happen many times.

I perform my gift on a regular basis, but I just don't speak up immediately. Sometimes I wait and discern if the message was really from the Holy Spirit.

I also have so many experiences in which I have lost some very important personal things and I will find it immediately after praying. Once, I lost a very important journal and I could not find it. I searched the entire house. Then after giving up searching for it, I stopped and prayed to God. I also asked for the intercession of St. Anthony since I knew St. Anthony is a saint known for helping people to find lost things. Then a thought will come to my mind that is the missing item, revealing that it was inside the cabinet next to my bed. And immediately when I opened the bedside cabinet, it was there.

Sometimes, I'll think about a friend whom I haven't talked for a long time and ask God to have this person call me or contact me because I lost their number. The person ends up calling me and telling me that she thought of me for some reason.

Also, I sense God as truly a living God who protects me all the time from all dangers, provides for my needs, especially in times of financial problems, and guides in our decisions.

Appendix 2

These are true testimonies told by my prayer partner of how she received the gift of healing messages through specific scriptures and Bible verses given to her by the Holy Spirit, as well as how she received the gift of tongues.

Please note: These testimonies were written by my prayer partner, so the first-person narrator "*I*" reflects her view.

Spiritual Messages Through Holy Scriptures (Holy Bible)

One of my spiritual gifts is to provide Holy Scriptures and Bible verses to people as led by the Holy Spirit. The Holy Spirit guides me to the scriptures located at various places in the Bible and in various sequences. The results are messages for the persons receiving them.

These scriptures are given for all sorts of reasons and mostly for confirming what the person already know. Sometimes the scriptures are for those who are sick to read and meditate upon. These scriptures do make them feel better.

I did not fully recognize this as a gift as I do today. When I was a young adult and throughout the years, I was led to scriptures in the Bible that pertained to certain circumstances. I would sometimes give or tell the scriptures to those in need, and some were messages for me. This gift was first confirmed to me through my prayer partner. Once this spiritual gift was further confirmed, I continued to be led by the Holy Spirit to provide certain persons a series of scriptures they were to read in the order given and only the ones provided. They would tell me the scriptures given to them were received and read as messages for them for confirmations, answers, and instructions from the Lord Jesus.

I was also told they needed the scriptures at the time sent to them. Most of the time, I did not know the reasons for the messages or even why the persons needed them. I just followed what the Holy Spirit led me to provide the persons. Sometimes I did not even hear back initially from the persons. I only did what I was led to do and let it go.

Through the grace of God, the Holy Spirit blessed me with the scriptures in the beginning of each chapter of the lessons in this book.

It is a blessing and comforting to know I am a vessel for the Lord, helping and uplifting those in need. It can be difficult at times when people seem to reject it or do not respond. I have learned now through the help of the Lord that it is not me who is doing it, but it is the Lord, and I am just His vessel.

The Gift of Tongues

The gift of tongues was given to me around 2007. One day, my younger sister and I were discussing the Bible when she brought up the topics of tongues and said, "You can speak in tongues, just pray, and ask the Lord." I got CDs from TV pastors on speaking tongues. After a few months, I began to speak in tongues intermittently.

On September 8, 2007, I went to a healing Mass in San Pedro, California. A priest from the Philippines was there who had the gift of healing since he was a young boy.

The priest went down the front row as we lined up laying hands and blowing on those who wanted healings and prayers. After he blew on me (my husband said he saw him blow on me), I fell back gently and to the floor. I began speaking in tongues continuously and loudly, my hands were open, and my arms went out straight to my sides like on a cross, my legs closed, and feet pointed down together.

This experience confirmed my gifts of tongues and it has continued ever since that time. Afterward, and during another time, I was out of town in Santa Barbara and was speaking to my prayer partner on the phone. She said she wanted to learn more about speaking tongues. The Holy Spirit had me start speaking in tongues, almost singing in tongues. My prayer partner said they sounded so beautiful. She sounded so happy to hear the gift of tongues.

The gift of tongues is truly a blessing in my life. I have since learned there are different types of tongues. I speak the same tongues but express in different ways, such as singing and praising, in smooth, delicate, loud, strong, and other ways. Spiritual gifts from God cannot be forced. Once you pray for them, the Holy Spirit comes upon you and you let go. It just simply happens at God's will.

To GOD be the Glory, in Jesus' name, Amen!

Appendix 3

These are true testimonies told by the author of how she received the gifts of prophecy and tongues.

The Spiritual Gift of Prophecy

I have had the spiritual gift of prophecy for over thirteen years. I hear Jesus through thoughts. I get assignments mostly through my morning prayers, and I perform my spiritual gift whenever Jesus tells me to. As I have mentioned throughout this book, I deliver messages to the prayer group members at our weekly Charismatic prayer group meetings. I also deliver messages to people wherever I go and when Jesus tells me to.

My very first message that I gave was to a minister who didn't know that he was going to receive one. It was awesome.

I remember for several weeks the minister had been on my mind. Thoughts would come about him, but I didn't write them down, and it didn't make that much sense to me at the time. Well, early on one Sunday morning close to one a.m. for the third time, I started getting thoughts that I knew were for him. I can't quite explain the feeling, but after the thoughts came three times real strong— "Stay the course, don't waver, only you know what God wants for you"—another thought came to me to write it down. So, I did.

As I wrote, I would have a thought and then I would write it. Then I would have another thought and again I had time to write it down before another thought would come. I did not paraphrase; I wrote this message from God exactly the way the thoughts came to me.

Stay the course, do not waver, only you know what God wants to tell you. One day, you will be on TV preaching the Word, not nationwide but worldwide. God has put a special anointing on you, and He has special things for you to do. You know what they are that He has for you. God has given you special talents to administer the Word to the people. Do not waver. Stay the course. You are the chosen one. You have special gifts from God. Stay the course. Do not waver. God has a lot in store for you. Stay the course. Do not waver. Do not give up. God has a plan for you. You will know because God will let you know. He has plans for you. This is a special message from God. You have prayed for the answer. This is the answer to your prayer.

I thanked God for allowing me to be the vessel, the instrument to give him His message. I was ever so humble and honored to give the minister such a special message from God.

I then prayed to God to let me know when to give him His message. The thought came: in the morning before he goes to church at seven a.m.

As I sat for a few minutes, thoughts continued to come, but this time the message was for me. My prophecy abilities are to give messages to people who need to know who have prayed for answers. I will relay the answers from God to the people who have prayed for the answers. I give them in different ways. I can give the answer by telling them. I can give them by helping them.

I went to sleep and woke up around seven a.m., calling and leaving messages for the minister to call me before he went to church. I was a little nervous at first because this was the first strong message from God that I was to tell the message. I have been working for years helping people. When people come to me for help, I already know they had prayed for help. This was the first time I told God's message, and I knew it would not be the last. I was happy that the minister accepted the message and knew it was true by what the message meant to him. He asked me to e-mail the message to him and I did.

I have since delivered messages to God's people in different ways. I have also continued to deliver messages to God's people in the Charismatic prayer group meetings held in my parish.

The Spiritual Gift of Tongues

I received the gift of tongues seven years ago during the Life in the Spirit Seminar (2009) at my parish church. The first time I ever wanted to speak tongues was when I was in one of the group activities during a discussion about speaking tongues. We later had a speaker who spoke on tongues and provided an atmosphere to receive the gift of tongues that night.

Below is an excerpt from my book, *Spiritual Awakening: Look What Happened to Me. Is It Happening to You Too?*

During Friday night's seminar (10/23/2009), we sang praising the Lord in the beginning. We prayed together. We prayed one decade of the Rosary. Our guest speaker for the evening spoke on the virtues and the seven gifts of the Holy Spirit. He mentioned several passages from the Bible such as Romans 1 and Isaiah 11:1. He also talked about speaking in tongues. There are different types. Sometimes you can speak another language or just sounds.

Father asked if anyone wanted the gift of speaking in tongues. I raised my hand and thought about asking Jesus if He wanted me to speak in tongues, so be it. For I was never truly drawn to speaking in tongues and very seldom heard of it. I didn't even know that Catholics spoke in tongues because my only encounters of hearing it before the seminar were people from other Christian religions.

The priest, whom we call "Father," said there are praying tongues and singing tongues. He told us that some people can also interpret tongues. He was going to show us the singing tongues. He had us to stand up and the person with the guitar played low music in the background as we sang a mantra of alleluia over and over until, if we were given the gift, we would start speaking in tongues.

So, I was singing "alleluia, alleluia, alleluia, alleluia," and then suddenly I started shouting in tongues. My eyes were closed, and I felt Father touch my shoulder and say, "Lower your voice so you can be with the group." I immediately lowered my voice to speak in tongues with the group. The ones who knew how to speak in tongues already did speak in tongues. I believe I was one of two given the gift of tongues that night. Praise the Lord!

After we finished, Father explained why I was shouting in tongues. He said, "Sometimes when it is your first time speaking in tongues, you shout out like casting out any demons or old, stressful stuff out of your body." I thanked him for mentioning it in front of the group. Father is blessed with the Holy Spirit. He is truly a vessel for Jesus.

After speaking in tongues, Father had us sit in the seats in the front row so that he could lay hands on us while we prayed for our family members. My prayer partner asked me to pray with her for the left side of her neck, her lower back, and her knees. She was always praying for the sick so I thought I would pray for her healing tonight.

I went up and quietly waited for Father to lay hands on me. I was so excited because I felt so blessed to have another opportunity for someone to lay hands on me. When Father touched my forehead, my head went back, my eyes were closed but were roaming around in their sockets, and my mouth was wide opened. I prayed for my prayer partner and her healing. I don't know how long I was in that position, but Father lifted my head and said in a soft voice to "keep my eyes close." So, I kept praying with my head bent down. It was a beautiful experience.

When we finished for the evening, the prayer leader came over to let me know that after the seminar program was over in November, they still met every Friday as a prayer group and offered me the opportunity to continue on afterwards. I thanked her for the opportunity, but I knew that

Jesus had a mission for me, and I would not know until Jesus gave me direction on which way to go.

She then took my hand and walked me over to the side away from the group that was socializing after the seminar and began to speak in tongues. I joined in and spoke tongues with her. When we finished, she said God wanted her to speak in tongues so that I would.

I remembered that during the seminar after we spoke in tongues, I asked Father, "When do we speak in tongues?" And in my head, I was wondering if I was going to even be able to remember how to since it was so new to me. He told me I could practice it in the shower, driving on my way to work, etc. He said I would eventually fit it into my daily prayers or routine of some kind. Before Father left, I asked him what I was saying, and he said I wasn't speaking a known language, it sounded like gibberish. Father did not have the gift of interpretation of tongues.

I thank Jesus for the gift of tongues. I had no idea that I would be speaking the gift of tongues that night. What an honor to speak to Jesus directly.

Thank you, Jesus. I love you.

References

Lesson 1: Preparation

Romans 11:29, 36
Romans 12:4–5,6–8,9–15, 16, 17, 18, 19–20, 21, 1–3
Romans. 13:1, 2, 3, 4, 5, 6–9, 10
1Corinthians 12:1–6, 7, 8–10, 11–13, 14–26, 27, 28, 29–31
Ephesians 3:20, 21
Galatians 5:25
John 10:21–28
Romans 13:1
Galatians 5:26
Romans 12:18
Luke 2:37
Acts 13:2–3
1 Corinthians 7:5
Matthew 6:16–18
1 Corinthians 7:26–27
2 Timothy 3:16–19
Galatians 5:22–25

Lesson 2: People

1 Corinthians 2:10–16
1 Corinthians 3:16–17
Corinthians 2:9
1 Corinthians 20, 2,22,23,3,4–6, 7–9,10–11
1 Corinthians 4:2, 6, 7
1 Corinthians 6:19–20
John 3:27, 30, 33–36
John 3:16–17
Mark 10:45
Matthew 25:35–36
Luke 10:1–5
Matthew 6:1–4
2 Timothy 3:16–17
Isaiah 55:11
John 8:1-5, 7, 9
1 Corinthians 4:5
Revelations 22:12

Lesson 3: Distribution

Matthew 18: 19, 20, 21, 22
Matthew 19:30 30
Matthew 21:21, 22
Matthew 20: 16
Matthew 22:32, 37–39
Matthew 25:40
Matthew 8:28, 29
Matthew 10:8, 20, 26, 27, 32, 33, 41
Matthew 13: 16–17
Matthew 14:27
Matthew 16:18–19
Matthew 19:26
Mark 8:34
Hebrews 2:4
Ephesians 4:1–6
1 Corinthians 12:7–10
1 Corinthians 12:11
Romans 12:1–2
James 1:2–4
Romans 11:29

Lesson 4: Faith

Matthew 11:11
Matthew 10:26–27, 32, 33, 19–20
Matthew 11:10
Matthew 9:2, 22, 28, 29Matthew 8:13
Matthew 10:8
Matthew 9:37–38
Matthew 7:1–2, 7, 12, 15, 17–18, 20, 24
Matthew 6:25, 32–34
Matthew 5:44, 46–48
Matthew 6:6
Matthew 5:12, 16
Matthew 4:19,
Isaiah 48:17
Hebrews 11:6
Romans 12:6–8
John 3:16
Mark 11:22–24
Matthew 21:22
Acts 2:38
John 15:7

Lesson 5: Dedication

Luke 1:30, 37, 38, 45, 79
Luke 3:16, 22
Luke 5:26
Luke 6:27, 28, 31, 32, 33, 36 37, 38
Luke 7:9, 23, 28, 50
Luke 8:5–8, 9–15, 17, 18
Luke 9:25
Luke 8:48, 50
Luke 9:6, 28, 29–31, 32, 33–35
Luke 10:20
Luke 11:9, 13
Luke 10:23–24
Luke 11:28
Luke 12:2–3,7,8–9, 10, 48, 43
Matthew 16:24–26
Matthew 16:26–27
Ephesians 2:10
Philippians 4:13
1 Corinthians 7:7
1 Corinthians 12:7–11
1 Peter 3:15
1 Peter 4:10–11

Lesson 6: Work

Psalms 103: 1–5
Psalms 107:1, 20 20
Psalms 118:8
Psalms 119:26, 27, 34–35
Psalms 118:21, 24, 29
Acts 8:14–15, 16–17, 35, 37–40
Acts 5:29, 32
Acts 9:1–14, 15–16, 17–20, 36, 37, 40–42
Acts 10:37–38, 40, 42, 43, 44
Acts 11:26B
Acts 13:2–6, 9
Acts 14:23
Acts 18:9–10
Acts 19:2,3–7, 11–12, 13–15
Acts 22:4, 6–16
Acts 16:30, 31–33
Romans 2:11
2 Timothy 1:6–7
2 Timothy 2:15
Matthew 6:16–18
1 John 5:14–15
2 Corinthians 10:13
1 Corinthians 6:19–20
Ephesians 2:10
1 Corinthians 12:4–7
1 Peter 4:10–11

Lesson 7: Listen

1 Samuel 8:4–5, 6,7, 10–18, 19, 22,
2 Kings 5:1, 9–10, 11–12, 13, 14–15
Isaiah 54:17
Isaiah 55:10–11
Isaiah 58:9–14
Isaiah 61:1–3
Isaiah 65:17–19
Isaiah 66:18
Jeremiah 1:5, 9, 17, 19
Jeremiah 7:23
Jeremiah 10:10
Jeremiah 11:5
Jeremiah 17:7–8, 10 Jeremiah 18:1, 6
Jeremiah 20:11, 13
John 14:26
John 16:13
Romans 8:11
Ephesians 6:18
1 Thessalonian 5:17
Romans 8:27
Ephesian 3:11
Romans 8:28
1 Corinthians 6:19
John 14:17

Lesson 8: Obedience

1 Samuel 24:6, 10
Mark 3: 14–15, 22, 23–26, 29
Mark 4:8, 11, 12, 14–20, 22, 24
Mark 5:2–5, 6–9, 10–13, 15, 25–29, 30, 34, 36
Mark 6:6, 12, 13
Mark 7:25–26, 27–28, 29–30, 32–34, 35
Mark 8:36
Mark 9:2–3, 4, 7, 17–18, 19, 20–21, 22, 23, 24, 25, 26–27, 28–29, 40, 41
Mark 10:9, 27
Mark 11:22, 23–24, 25–26
Mark 12:12, 29–31
Mark 13:11, 37
Titus 3:11
Luke 6:46–47
John 15:14
Matthew 7:21
Acts 5:29
1 Peter 1:2
Luke 11:28
James 1:22–25
Romans 6:16–17

Lesson 9: Ministry

Mark 6:7, 13
Mark 1:23–24, 25, 26–27, 28
Mark 3:22, 23–26
Mark 9:17–22, 23–25, 26, 28, 29
Luke 10:17, 20, 21, 23–24
Luke 11:14, 15, 17–21, 24–26, 28
Luke 12:2–3, 4–5, 13, 30, 48
Luke 14:11, 14
Luke 15:9–10
Luke 16:21
Luke 18:27
1 Peter 4:10
1 Corinthians 12:1
1 Corinthians 14:40
Acts 6:4
Romans12:4–8
1 Corinthians 12:11
Romans 12:6
Colossians 3:23–24
2 John 1:8
Hebrews 10:35
Romans 8:28

Lesson 10: Spirituality

Mark 6:4–5, 7, 10–12, 12–13
Matthew 10:19, 20, 26, 32, 33, 41
Matthew 9:22, 28, 29
Matthew 10:8
Matthew 9:37–38
Matthew 7:2-5, 7, 12
Matthew 16:23
Matthew 17:2-3, 7, 14–19, 20–21
Matthew 18:18, 19, 20
Matthew 19:26
Matthew 21:22
Matthew 22:14
Ephesians 6:12–13
James 4:7
Ephesians 6:10–17
2 Corinthians 5:21
Ephesians 6:14
2 Corinthians 5:21
Ephesians 6:14
2 Timothy 2:15
Ephesians 6:16
1 Peter 1:5
Ephesians 6:17
Hebrews 4:12–13
Ephesians 6:15
Colossians 3:15
2 Corinthians 10:35
2 Corinthians 3:17
2 Peter 2:16
2 Samuel 22:2
Psalms 40:13
James 4:7
John 8:32

Lozano, Neal *Unbound* A Practical Guide to Deliverance Chosen Books, Grand Rapids, MI 2003. 2010

Sears, Fr. M. The *Charism of Tongues,* Queenship Publishing Company, Goleta, CA 2008.

Renner, Rick You *Don't Have To Take It Anymore Because You Are…DRESSED TO KILL A Biblical Approach To Spiritual Warfare And Armor*, Harrison House, Tulsa, OK. 1991

ABOUT THE AUTHOR

Jacqueline Parker Scott, Ed.D., M.B.A. earned a doctorate from Pepperdine University and a master's degree in business administration from Golden Gate University. She has been a lecturer in the Los Angeles Community College District since 1997 and an associate professor at Santa Monica College since 1999. Dr. Jacquie is also a parenting education instructor since 1994. She has co-authored a parenting education book with her daughter, Olympia Scott, *Super Parenting: Raising the Next Generation.* Dr. Jacquie also authored, *Spiritual Awakening: Look What Happened to Me. Is it Happening to You Too?*

Made in the USA
Columbia, SC
20 March 2022

57869756R00121